"Julie and Daren obviously k
'right' thing to do is when it ,
lent read for anyone in a leadership role. The stories are both insightful and over-the-top humorous, and the lessons learned go on and
on. You will easily gain as much common sense to apply to your own
dealings with people, in countless situations, as with any management
book on the market today."

—John A. Wright, Former Vice President Human Resources,
Layne Christensen Company and Partner, Beyond HR Solutions

"I believe that true leadership in the workplace starts within each person who is empowered to make a difference. The authors of *Lifeguard,
Babysitter, Executioner* provide a great backdrop from which to learn
about best practices for managing people to become empowered,
along with ideas on how to create a dynamic corporate culture—one
person at a time. The stories provide viewpoints from many different
seats within an organization, all of which provide a new perspective
on the importance of an organization's most precious resource—its
human capital."

—Dan Bailey, Former President and COO, CARSTAR

"This book will save you from many hard knocks that might otherwise come your way while managing people. Whether in a corporate
environment, a university setting, or any other work location, you
will find practical tips on managing a workforce that are infused with
large doses of wisdom, insight, and common sense. Your people skills
will be heightened—all while being wildly entertained!"

—Tamra Wilson Setser, Former Associate Dean, University of
Missouri School of Law and Partner, Armstrong Teasdale LLP

Lifeguard, Babysitter, Executioner

A Real-World Guide to Hiring, Firing
& Building a Winning Workforce

Daren Fristoe, J.D. & Julia R. McKee, J.D.

RIVER GROVE
BOOKS

Published by River Grove Books
Austin, Texas
www.rivergrovebooks.com

Copyright ©2014 DJ Global Publishing, LLC

Distributed by Greenleaf Book Group LLC

For ordering information or special discounts for bulk purchases, please contact Greenleaf Book Group LLC at PO Box 91869, Austin, TX 78709, 512.891.6100.

Design and composition by Greenleaf Book Group LLC
Cover design by Greenleaf Book Group LLC
Cover images: ©iStockphoto.com/©O'Luk
⠀⠀⠀⠀⠀⠀⠀⠀⠀©iStockphoto.com/©Tashatuvango
⠀⠀⠀⠀⠀⠀⠀⠀⠀©iStockphoto.com/©yaytsoo

Publisher's Cataloging-In-Publication Data
Fristoe, Daren.
⠀ Lifeguard, babysitter, executioner : a real-world guide to hiring, firing & building a winning workforce / Daren Fristoe & Julia McKee.—1st ed.
⠀⠀ p. ; cm.
⠀ Issued also as an ebook.
⠀ ISBN: 978-1-938416-75-0

⠀ 1. Personnel management. 2. Employee selection. 3. Employees—Dismissal of.
4. Supervision of employees. I. McKee, Julia. II. Title.
HF5549 .F75 2014
658.31⠀⠀⠀⠀⠀⠀⠀⠀⠀⠀⠀⠀⠀⠀⠀⠀⠀⠀⠀⠀⠀⠀⠀⠀⠀⠀⠀⠀⠀⠀⠀⠀2013949506

Printed in the United States of America
First Edition

Contents

Foreword

Hi! I'm Hollywood's Rob Riggle, star of stage and screen and runner up for *People Magazine's* sexiest man alive for the past ten years*. I'm so honored that my sister asked me to write a foreword for her first book. Julie McKee, my sister, is the co-author of *Lifeguard, Babysitter, and Executioner*. My sister is outstanding . . . maybe one of the most amazing people I've ever had the privilege of knowing, and I live in Hollywood (see above) so you can imagine how great the people are that I meet.

Seriously, though . . . I had to say "seriously though" because this is a business book. Let's talk about this book for a moment, shall we? Daren and Julie have put together a book that contains all the practical tools any manager, director, V.P. or CEO would need to lead their organization with confidence. Before I became an international superstar, I was just an average person, like you**. I was an officer in the United States Marine Corps and also worked briefly in corporate America. I wish this book would have existed when I was leading people. I would have saved myself a ton of stress and many unnecessary mistakes.

Anyone who is responsible for leading an organization or hopes to lead an organization needs to read this book and keep a copy within arms reach throughout the remainder of their career.

*Not True.

**More like below average.

Julie is one of the smartest, most hardworking, and logical people I've ever known. If she says this is the way to do something, take it to the bank. She always does her research, she always explores the options and she is consistently seeking the best solution to whatever problems may arise. Her thirst for knowledge and desire to learn and experience all she can has made her one of the most sought-after HR professionals in the Midwest. She has seen it all . . . in the courtroom and in the boardroom.

Growing up, Julie was basically perfect. This, of course, is coming from her little brother who was constantly in trouble. However, as biased as my opinion may be, it's still very accurate. She's always had a wonderful logic and a very insightful understanding of human nature. She's nobody's fool, but her compassion for people, even idiots, is what makes her the perfect balance of "tough" lawyer and admired leader.

I don't know Daren nearly as well, but if my sister thought enough of him to write a book with him, he is good to go.

Lifeguard, Babysitter, and Executioner is a blueprint for any leader that has the responsibility of leading, guiding, advising, and reprimanding subordinates. This book should sit on every executive's desk and should be well worn. It will be the reference guide you will use on a weekly basis as long as you are working.

I hope you enjoy this book. I hope you learn from this book. I trust my sister and so can you. She and Daren have given you a wonderful gift in this book; please take advantage.

Semper Fidelis,
Lt. Col. Rob Riggle, USMCR RET.
Actor, Comedian, Writer . . . Google it . . .

Preface

As with many good things in life, this book came together in a very serendipitous way. It is the product of two long-time professionals with complimentary backgrounds whose paths converged: one author (Daren) with corporate human resources experience and also armed with a law degree, the other author (Julie) with extensive legal practice experience and also working in the corporate human resources field. We decided to create something from our shared experiences in the trenches of the workplace and the benches of the courtroom, using a blend of humor and takeaway value for our readers.

Our audience for this book includes anyone who has ever managed or been managed by another person in the workplace, anyone who owns their own business and hires at least one other person, anyone who has ever had any direct or indirect management responsibilities, anyone who has worked in or near the field of human resources (HR), and anyone who has ever been housed in a corner office, with the word "chief" in their job title. By our calculations, that means roughly 95 percent of the entire workforce are potential readers of our book!

Does the world really need another book about HR-related topics such as interviewing, hiring, and coaching? The answer we found, of course, was a resounding yes. Especially a book with a twist, like the one you're holding now. With more than forty years of professional proficiency between us, our collective knowledge and experience have resulted in this revelation of common themes of employee behavior (ranging from slightly unusual to downright unacceptable), management skills (ranging from nonexistent, to poor, to on-the-fly), and corporate culture (ranging from . . . wait a minute, *what* culture?).

We know (with tongue firmly in cheek) that you, as our target audience, can relate to some of the stories we've presented, and we hope you can use the lessons delivered at the end of each chapter to help you become a better practitioner in the fine science of managing human capital. Thank you for spending your time with us. You'll be so glad you did.

Acknowledgments

There are so many people to thank for the inspiration in creating this book. The professional journeys that we have been on thus far, our good fortune in working with extraordinary people, and the humorous situations (along with some slightly odd behaviors) that have provided the backdrop for this work are invaluable. So to each of you (and you know who you are), former and current colleagues, peers, managers, executives, mentors, and friends, a special "THANK-YOU."

We are grateful for the team of people that helped make this project a reality. Our marketing and public relations team of Paul Evans and Sara Paxton of Evans Media Group for their guidance through the creative and publishing process. Jon McKee of Jon McKee Photography, whose pictures made us look better than we really are in person. Many thanks to our second and third sets of editing eyes from colleagues Lauren Claflin, Lisa Moseley, and Kris Melcher. And a very heartfelt thank-you to Rob Riggle, for contributing to this book with his customary flair and humorous wit to which we aspire.

On a more personal note, nothing is possible without the

love and support of our family and friends. From tireless reading of the material, to conspicuously fake laughter at our attempted humor, and never-ending patience, your support has proven to be priceless. We love you all beyond words—and you know we have a lot of 'em.

    —*Daren and Julie*

To my wife and best friend Jody, thank you for always being there. Your love, compassion, humor, intelligence, creativity, and positive reinforcement all make ours a lasting partnership. I am a better person with you in my life and I look forward to every day with you.

    To my fantastic kids, Adam and Emma, you are incredible sources of strength and vision, making my life more meaningful. You inspire me to seek greater heights, while keeping in mind what's really important. You continue to amaze me and I could not be more proud of who you are. Together we make an unbeatable team! Love you always.

    To Mom and Dad, thank you for your lifelong support of me and my dreams. When you spoke, I listened (not at first, of course, but later when I was more mature). Growing up, our home provided me with a solid foundation, allowing me to focus on family and community and serving others.

    Finally, a special thank-you to my late grandmother, Elsie. From my time with her, I witnessed true quality of character, integrity, a hard work ethic, and the unequivocal love of family. I can only hope to measure up to some of her high standards. Thanks, Grandma, for everything you taught me.

    —*Daren*

To my wonderful husband, Mark—thank you for being both a cheerleader and a coach (at the right times). You never stop believing, even when I do. Your love and encouragement mean the world to me. I love you.

To my remarkable daughters, Mallory, Chandler, and Brooke—you inspire me and fill me with tremendous joy. I am so proud of each of you—you are kind, genuine, and extraordinary young women. I love you beyond measure and believe in you without limits.

To my *favorite* brother, Rob—you've made me laugh from the start. Thank you for your love, laughter, and brotherly advice. I'm *your* biggest fan.

To my amazing parents, Robert and Sandra—you've given me *roots* and *wings* that were deep enough to weather any storm and strong enough to support any dream. I cherish every lesson you've taught me. You opened doors. You led by example. Your strength and guidance are immeasurable.

—*Julie*

Introduction

Lifeguard, Babysitter, Executioner. These are three roles that managers, executives, business owners, and human resource professionals fill from time to time in their careers. Depending on your position in the company, you may already have experience in all three, likely with varying levels of success. Were you trained to handle the oddities of employee behavior? Doubtful. Is it remotely possible to be prepared for everything an employee can dream up today or tomorrow or the next day? No. That said, by reading this book, you will be ready for a broad range of issues and concerns, because it is likely that our stories closely resemble what has happened in your company, and our tools are ones you will be able to implement to help alleviate challenging situations.

When we began writing this book, the overriding idea was to focus on our list of "Top 10" Human Resources topics, including: recruiting, interviewing, hiring, conducting performance appraisals, handling employee development and retention, providing employee recognition, coaching, addressing workplace harassment, handling management processes, and termination of employment.

We chose to align each of the Top 10 topics with the applicable role—Lifeguard, Babysitter, or Executioner—so you will see the chapters set forth accordingly. In part I, the Lifeguard section, we address the workplace topics of recruiting, interviewing, hiring, and onboarding. These HR roles are akin to the watchful eye and vigilant protection provided by a lifeguard who must set the rules and be prepared to oversee the welfare of everyone in the water (workplace). We divided the Babysitter role into two sections: In the first (part II), we speak to workforce matters such as performance management, employee retention and development, and employee recognition programs, much like the care a babysitter provides when setting expectations for a child and providing feedback on matters handled well or poorly by the child (employee). In the second Babysitter section (part III), the role refers to the tasks of successful coaching, honing management skills, and addressing inappropriate workplace behavior. This is similar to a babysitter's duty to help children master new skills and refine their behaviors. Finally, part IV, the Executioner section, provides information about bringing one's employment to an end and "executing" upon employment terminations, which is likely the most unpleasant HR duty known to anyone. (Yes, some may dread the task as if they were having to deliver a death sentence.)

Each chapter is divided into three sections to provide a framework to move through the topic more easily, and for ease of use in referring to the material as a workplace resource. The three sections and their uses are:

- **Tales: Am I the only sane person in the room?** Sometimes humorous, sometimes unbelievable, always instructive stories about the workplace.

- **Tips: What else do I need to know?** Helpful background information and discerning insights on the topic at hand.

- **Tactics: Where do I go from here?** This is the secret sauce. Here you will find practical advice providing you with tactical ideas, tools, and processes to implement.

We don't intend for you to place this book on your office shelf, spine out, never to be touched again after you've read it. In the truest sense of the word, this is a *workbook*, with workplace situations to note and real-world solutions to use. While you read each chapter, think about your own experiences, current or past, and picture how you would act or react given the situations described. We will have done our job if your book has dog-eared pages and highlighted text when you reach the end.

So in for a penny, in for a pound? Let's get started.

Note: We have not addressed the specific nuances related to a unionized workforce throughout this book. The matters discussed herein are presumed to be in a non-union setting.

Part I

LIFEGUARD

Let's start at the beginning of the employment life cycle with recruiting, interviewing, hiring, and onboarding. As any good lifeguard (or HR professional) would do, grab a life preserver and prepare to assess the best and worst swimmers (job candidates) in the pool, along with identifying the strongest swimmers. The pool will also need to be prepared and ground rules set for everyone's first day in the sun (on the job).

CHAPTER 1

Attracting Talent to Your Door

CRYSTAL BALLS & PALM READING COME IN HANDY

I hire people brighter than me and then I get out of their way.
—Lee Iacocca

We decided to start this book with advice on how to attract the most talented candidates for your organization. This approach seems logical enough. Attracting solid talent to our door and, ultimately, hiring that (nearly) perfect talent is one of our callings as business professionals. In fact, it may be our highest calling. Do you hear the celestial chorus ringing in your ears?

With the continuing changes in the employment market and talent pool, HR professionals must be adaptable enough to manage casting the net effectively, weeding out unworthy candidates quickly, and setting up a screening and interview process that secures Mr. or Mrs. Right (or, as the circumstances require, Mr. or Mrs. Right Now). Today's marketplace offers a surplus of both qualified and overqualified job candidates. This means that in the current climate most job openings will have a number of candidates who meet the minimum requirements. As a result, the hiring manager doesn't have to settle for a "nearly qualified" candidate anymore. Your evaluation of the candidate's suitability for the job may go well beyond minimum requirements into more subjective factors such as initiative, integrity, and whether the candidate is a good culture-fit. (We will slice and dice the selection process in chapter 2.)

Tales: Am I the only sane person in the room?

Throughout the book, we will refer to two bosses. So there's no mistaken identity, we will refer to them as "Good Boss" and "Bad Boss" (clever, right?). You've likely met both of them in your career. Good Boss is an effective leader whose regular exercise of wise counsel and sound judgment is notable. Bad Boss is, quite simply, the opposite.

While you are busy polishing your crystal ball or otherwise preparing to yield an amazing crop of talented recruits, Good Boss has commissioned an all-out offensive to put a full-court press on attracting the best job candidates that can be found.

Unfortunately, Bad Boss (to whom you report) initiates the recruitment effort from a glass-half-empty perspective. Bad Boss comes to you and says, "(Insert HR lackey name here), why don't we have any candidates for the new position?" During this professionally intimate moment, voices in your head are responding, "You mean the position I don't know about?" or "You mean the position we don't really need?" or, simply, "What?" Then reality rears its ugly head, and you remember you are (insert HR lackey name here) and you dive on your well-worn sword, apologizing and committing to get it done. Many obvious challenges come with blindly saying yes to Bad Boss and making such a commitment, but what choice do you have? None, really.

If you are the one tasked with attracting people to add to the team, you have to assess what obstacles the company may be facing and what opportunities best respond to those obstacles. Based on Bad Boss's directive to have candidates available ASAP for a position that you either didn't know existed or didn't know needed filling, you must now stop with business-as-usual and pull out the crystal ball or resort to palm reading. If you decide to go with palm reading, at least you've got lines to follow.

Tips: What else do I need to know?

To attract talent, really good talent, we must be cognizant of obstacles and think outside the box (the Help Wanted advertisement box, that is) to be creative in seeking solutions for the particular occasion. First, the obstacles. Next, the solutions. Then, how to execute.

To determine the obstacles, you must answer the question, "What stands in the way of that super-perfect candidate finding you and being interested in your offer of employment?" If, in fact, something does stand in the way, what can you do about it? A good place to start in evaluating the attractiveness of employment with your organization is to consider the following factors to determine your strengths and weaknesses:

- The job

- Corporate culture (values, mission statement, goals)

- Work environment (casual, professional, warehouse)

- Compensation and benefits package

- Opportunity for advancement

- Location of the business

- The business's public reputation

- Benefits or paid-time-off packages

- Job perks (free coffee, wellness programs, concierge services)

- Worksite amenities (fitness center, on-site day care)

- Days or hours of operation

- Flexibility of work schedule

- Professional development (training courses, tuition reimbursement)

- Telecommuting

- Work satisfaction (personal growth, performance feedback, goal setting)

- Dress code

- The industry

- Management team

- Company size

- Company situation (start-up venture; Fortune Top-50)

None of these items in and of themselves are necessarily good or bad. The impact of these factors is largely reliant upon the eye of the beholder. It is truly amazing what may or may not be important to job candidates. A candidate may view one item negatively, yet that item may be the very thing to seal the deal with the next. We are sure you are aware of the generational "buckets" that create today's multigenerational workforce. These buckets bear repeating here as they relate to candidates' internal wiring and generational DNA, which influence their decision making. (NOTE: The following definitions are hybrids and paraphrased from multiple sources. Don't kill the messenger.)

- **Baby Boomers:** Born during the post–World War II boom, roughly 1946 to 1960, those in this category have been identified as participating at a greater rate in higher education and exhibiting a "success through hard work" persona.

- **Gen X:** Born between 1961 and 1981, this grouping blends the Baby Boomers' classroom-training background (i.e., long division, direct communication, hands-on approach) with the Gen Y world of speed, technological advances, and less personal interaction. Gen X, for obvious reasons, can often find themselves as mediators between the Boomers and the Gen Y group.

- **Gen Y:** Born between 1981 and 2001, this grouping (also known as the Millennial Generation or Millennials) has grown up under the glow of the Internet, cell phones, and iPods, with expectations of job advancement and learning new skills at a more rapid rate than their more senior colleagues.

Even armed with a magic wand, HR cannot tweak the various job elements discussed above to satisfy each of the generational buckets. But HR can do two things to attract the best talent for the given job:

1. Carefully communicate the specific elements of the job to ensure each candidate is fully apprised of the requirements of the position, the work environment, and job expectations. Nothing should be left to chance.

2. Communicate the job opening in a way that appeals to multiple generations whenever possible.

Take a factor from the list that can't be changed—let's say location of the worksite—and let's put your worksite about twenty minutes outside of town in a hard-to-reach place. Determine what perks make up for the inconvenient location, and focus on those. Perhaps it's a really cool lunchroom with subsidized, tasty food and a high-tech, coffee-shop atmosphere. This means convenience and savings for your Baby Boomers, who want to stay on task throughout the day with minimal disruption. This means a place to relate with colleagues and to recharge for your Gen Xers. This means a place to unplug with iTunes and grab a latte for your Gen Y population. Get it? Position your solution to meet the audience's needs. It's still the same lunchroom, but it can fill different needs.

Or maybe it's an on-site fitness center, or flexible Fridays, or getting a half-day vacation on your birthday. Whatever the perk(s), there is *something* that will likely tip the scale in your favor.

COMMUNICATING YOUR OFFERINGS

There are remarkable solutions for recruiting today that are based on methodologies from back in the day. Decades ago, BI (Before Internet), HR professionals tasked with finding new talent would place a Help Wanted ad in a newspaper, commission a headhunter (sorry, "search firm"), set up a booth at a career fair, work with school placement offices, put a sign in the window, fan the flames of their own network—or a combination of these. There were other methods, but these were the most prevalent and, of course, the return on investment (ROI) varied among them.

Many of these methods are still used today, but in variations that offer better cost-benefit results. For instance, Help Wanted ads still exist, but they are placed in the virtual world. Talk about ROI—many virtual advertising venues involve no cost. Companies now advertise job openings on their own websites, on LinkedIn or Facebook pages, or on selected professional association sites that post job openings as a service to their members. Job candidates now handle a significant amount of the heavy lifting on their own by conducting job searches through online job boards, job aggregator sites, career portals on company sites, and their own networking through social media and search engine searches.

Biz Tip   Put yourself in the job candidate's shoes. How and where will the job seeker go to find a job opening like yours? Go to those places.

If you're seeking a larger pool of candidates for a generalist or entry-level position, place your job advertisement on a widely known site like CareerBuilder or Monster.com or through the online postings in the local newspaper. If you are seeking a high-level professional position, use professional association website postings and job boards. There is often a fee to post, but you will be face-to-face (in the virtual sense) with a very targeted audience of people. Your candidate pool will be more narrow, and you will reach the people you're truly looking for.

Search firms remain a viable alternative in the recruiting business, and many of these outsourced recruiting solutions are turning to high-tech strategies to get the job done. We recently worked with a company that is a vibrant, small start-up tech business. The company was recruiting for salespeople with knowledge of a highly technical and specific nature. It was important to quickly find these direct salespeople internationally. This was best executed through a search firm with feet on the ground in those markets, which included the United Kingdom, Germany, Italy, France, and Switzerland. Upon selecting two qualified firms, the company decided that the up-front cost (and contingent fee upon successful placement in one case) of this global search for the proverbial needle in the haystack was well worth the money. We are not suggesting that you walk yourself or your internal recruiting colleague out the door by outsourcing. We are simply suggesting that it may be a viable alternative in the right situation.

Also, depending on the consistency of an organization's hiring needs, there might be an increase in its ROI through RPO. (Huh?) Recruitment process outsourcing, or RPO, refers to an outsourced recruiting solution in which a business may shift some or all of its recruiting needs to an outside provider. Typically, the contracts involve a base monthly fee that can be adjusted up or down relative to the services utilized and the number of searches conducted. A business can start small and build from there. A company may decide to use RPO in limited circumstances, such as only for professional-level hires or select services. However, the menu of services can be extensive. If existing staff are already performing these services, a business may also find that it can have its cake and eat it too. Often, when RPO is being considered, the business finds ways to use the existing staff more strategically while off-loading more transactional or administrative functions. In other cases, if positions are eliminated, "re-badging" may occur wherein the outside vendor may hire the displaced worker(s).

Biz Tip   Recruiting functions include sourcing applicants, screening and background checks, selection management, job offers, strategic hiring analysis, and onboarding. Each recruiting function should be evaluated to determine whether it can be most effectively handled by internal staff or external resources.

Just one more thing about outsourcing: Many search firms create virtual communities for job seekers. Here, job seekers and job providers may find each other. These virtual communities are also established through local associations, non-profit groups, or churches that aid members through online resources.

Your organization can also initiate the conversation by using a company-sponsored blog, Twitter account, or website portal to communicate your job openings. To go old school for a moment, this is the Help Wanted sign in the front window; it's just that now the "window" is virtual. To do this right, grab people from each generational bucket (careful not to cross into age-based comments or stereotypes when doing so) and obtain their input to describe the job. (The manager's input has already been gathered, of course.) This multigenerational input can also be used to create recruiting communications about the company's culture, reasons to work there, or other meaningful commentary that will attract talent that is right for the organization. It's your organization's message. Make it real. Be authentic.

You'll recognize that all of these are just back-in-the-day methodologies cloaked in high-tech functionality. Glad-handing at Rotary Club meetings is now called LinkedIn. Career fairs are now online job boards. Networking is initiated through online introductions.

Tactics: Where do I go from here?

We've discussed the old, new, and blended schools of thought for recruiting and high-tech strategies to use to attract talented candidates. Ultimately, the ability to effectively attract qualified candidates will require your organization to adopt a targeted approach that satisfies your business needs and also melds with your business operations. It's time to create tools that reinforce both the value and the methodology of attracting top-notch, relevant candidates to your company. We've touched on these already, but we want to take this opportunity to summarize them in three points for ease of use.

1. **Recruiting communications.** The written and verbal communications that relate to each job opening must be clear and well-defined. Input from key management about the tasks to be performed, responsibilities to be

assumed, and duties to be handled must be gathered. Ask yourself:

—Are our current recruiting efforts yielding quality candidates with applicable experience and skills?

—Is there a satisfactory alignment of the skills required for the job and the candidates who are responding?

If the answer for both questions is no, check the clarity of the job advertisement and related communications. Make sure that anything related to the attraction of candidates is clearly defined, approved by the appropriate parties, and stated consistently throughout the process. First and foremost, be sure the job posting is clear. Nothing is more embarrassing than an inaccurate portrayal of the job title or job duties in a job post—except a misstatement of the level of compensation in communications with the candidate. An accurate description of the job itself is the most effective way to ensure you attract the most qualified and relevant candidates from the start.

Biz Tip   Ensure clarity of job-related information in your recruiting communications. Be consistent!

2. **Recruiting tools.** As we stated earlier, there is a level of ROI analysis that must be used when casting the net. There are both expensive and inexpensive ways to

find candidates, but your organization must decide the approach that best fits the circumstance. Ask yourself:

—What are the budget and the time frame for filling this position?

—Is this the only position to be filled?

—What is the overall hiring forecast for the next twelve months?

—Is this a one-and-done search, or are we also gathering résumés for future reference to build an applicant pipeline in the battle for qualified talent?

Our best high-tech recruiting tool is only as effective as the need it's trying to fill. This is a dynamic target, and there is not a one-size-fits-all solution. From a LinkedIn job posting to a global search using RPO, the right answer will ultimately be determined by an analysis of the specific recruiting goal and alignment of that goal with the high-tech recruiting resources.

Biz Tip   High-tech recruiting tools are plentiful. Know your goal. Be selective!

3. **Recruiting roadblocks.** Anticipate the points that might hinder your organization's recruiting efforts, then prepare a plan to overcome and impress. Remember the adage "The best offense is a good defense."

Using the lunchroom example we gave earlier in this chapter, prepare your organization to put its best foot forward and make a lasting impression from the start. Ask yourself:

—What might keep a qualified candidate from accepting our job offer?

—What else would I want to know if I were a candidate
  for this job?

—What else should a qualified candidate know before
  accepting the job?

Make a list of the least desirable characteristics associated with the particular job opening. It could be a job function (cleaning out garbage dumpsters) or related job attribute (a flat organization with fewer opportunities for growth). Prepare a mental list of rebuttals, direct and indirect, as well as a list of positive qualities that are otherwise present in the job and/or company. For example, to the candidate whose job involves cleaning garbage dumpsters, it is important to know the company also offers a top-notch benefit package, every other Friday is a shortened workday, and eligibility for a pay raise kicks in after only six months of employment. To the job candidate concerned about a flat organization, there may be upsides such as more opportunity to work autonomously, fewer layers of required approvals, and the ability to effectuate change more rapidly. Hmm, all this doesn't sound half bad.

Biz Tip   Identify potential recruiting roadblocks. Prepare your glass-is-half-full speech. Be genuine!

BOTTOM LINE

Today's marketplace is bursting with qualified talent. Consider all of the recruiting tools at your disposal and select those that best suit the goals of the organization and the needs of the job opening. The answer may differ depending on the job, so be prepared to ask yourself the questions from above—over and over. Also use the recruiting process as an outward-facing opportunity to promote the best attributes of your organization. You'll find the right people, even without a crystal ball or palm reading, by being intentional and using the right recruiting tactic for the particular position. You'll be so glad you did.

CHAPTER 2

The Lost Art of Conducting Effective Interviews

HIRING THE PERFECT CANDIDATE EVERY TIME & OTHER PACKS OF LIES

*The single biggest problem with communication
is the illusion that it's taken place.*
—George Bernard Shaw

You've attracted talented candidates to fill a particular job opening in your company, so now it's time to focus solely on the adventure of interviewing them. Why do we consider this a lost art? By "lost art" we are referring to two distinctive characteristics of interviews that we have seen change over the course of our careers: One is the element of time, actually the lack thereof, and the resulting lack of preparation prior to an interview. The other change relates to the information-gathering process itself. Interviewers previously relied on what the interviewee actually said in an interview, whereas now interviewers can access data about an applicant without the applicant's involvement. (Think Google searches, Facebook homepages, and LinkedIn employment chronologies.) Both of these changes—diminished interview prep and independent data collection—may result in interviewers shortchanging themselves or the candidates in the process.

First, let us say that very few things are as rewarding in our profession as identifying the ideal candidate for a job, creating the environment and opportunity for the new employee's success, and then witnessing the positive results. Effective interviewing provides a framework in which all parties involved (the candidate, the hiring manager, HR, and upper management) can create a dynamic and meaningful dialogue that results in a mutually beneficial outcome.

Tales: Am I the only sane person in the room?

It poses an interesting challenge when untrained or unprepared people within your organization conduct interviews. The unwitting interviewer may be naive about the potential pitfalls (i.e., illegal questions) or may reflect poorly on your company without any ill intent whatsoever. Also, be on the lookout for the "all-over-the-map" interviewer within your ranks whose interview dialogue strays so far afield that you may never fully recover from the experience.

We are going to reference Bad Boss again as we retell some of the finer interviewing experiences we've witnessed (er . . . heard about). Please raise your hand if any of these scenarios sound eerily familiar.

BAD BOSS ASKS THE CANDIDATE WHATEVER HE WANTS

We are in Bad Boss's conference room—just the job candidate, the boss, and me (Daren), the HR pro. I would guess that most of my colleagues, as well as most of the planet, understand that there are questions you cannot legally ask. These are the questions—about age, race, national origin, religion, sex, and so forth—that are not job relevant and have no bearing on anything other than exposing a momentary lapse of good judgment.

Roughly twenty minutes into the interview, Bad Boss looked the candidate in the eye and said, "You're Jewish, aren't you?" I had my first professional out-of-body experience. I truly felt the room close in and saw the balance of my career flash before my eyes (knowing that allowing Bad Boss to speak in such a manner would be in some perverse way *my fault*). The candidate looked at me, knowing we were in clearly inappropriate waters, and answered, "Yes, I am."

Thinking we were somehow past the crisis, I exhaled, but Bad Boss didn't skip a beat in adding a follow-up comment. "That's good, because you people know fabric." After the interview, the candidate assured me he was not offended by Bad Boss's impropriety, but I decided to focus on just how much of a signing bonus I was going to pay him for his silence.

BAD BOSS MAKES CANDIDATES CRY

We are in the corporate boardroom, and Bad Boss wants to interview candidates for the open comptroller position. The first candidate joins us. She is extremely polished and professional, and is on paper and in reputation exactly what I thought we wanted. As Bad Boss begins to review the candidate's résumé for the first time—in front of her—he notices in the work history section that three companies in a row had gone out of business. Asking the obvious, "What happened at Companies X, Y, and Z?" Bad Boss positioned himself closer to the candidate, who now would not make eye contact. When she explained clearly what had occurred at each company (a merger, the death of the owner, and a business closure), I assumed her answer was satisfactory, as did she.

But Bad Boss felt the need to say, "You must be the *black widow*, leaving behind such a *trail of dead companies*." As the woman began to cry, I handed her the tissue box and Bad Boss excused himself, telling me the interview was over. Needless to say, she didn't get hired, but at least Bad Boss felt better.

BAD BOSS LIKES TO TALK

In this last tale, Bad Boss, the candidate, and I were in a common lobby area for the interview. Why there, you may ask? Because Bad Boss said so! You can picture the chaos, of course. People were passing by on a regular basis, trading acknowledging glances or pleasantries with Bad Boss as he halfheartedly tried to make conversation with the candidate—to no avail.

My role in this situation is to somehow move the interview to a conclusion and get some feedback, positive or negative, from Bad Boss as to whether to go forward or keep looking. After *three hours* of sitting in this busy lobby, listening to Bad Boss speak about himself and his vision and the company at large (but never asking the candidate any questions), the interview ended. The candidate had barely said a word—not by choice but by design. This particular Bad Boss typically made hiring decisions based on résumé and reputation, not from information that could be gathered and evaluated from an interview.

Much to our collective surprise, Bad Boss extended the offer on the spot, and the candidate said yes. All I could think, however, was, *There went another three hours of my life I won't get back*.

In each scenario, you witnessed Bad Boss characteristics being carried out by otherwise well-intentioned leaders. Let's move beyond these examples and discuss the right way to interview.

Tips: What else do I need to know?

Let's start with the initial interaction between the company's representative (this could be the hiring manager, HR, or another designated individual) and the potential candidate. From the start, this interaction involves a critical moment that can make or break the relationship. As with everything we do, there are right ways, not-so-right ways, and very wrong ways to operate. Here's our recommended road map for the right way to handle the initial screening and interview process.

INITIAL SCREENING OF RÉSUMÉS AND/OR APPLICATIONS

This responsibility requires the reviewer to analyze the information provided by the job candidate to determine if the candidate's skills, experience, and education meet the minimum criteria set for the job opening. Those who don't meet the minimum criteria can be eliminated from further consideration. Pay attention to the little stuff: misspellings, poor grammar, and sloppiness. Remember, this is every applicant's first attempt to impress you. How'd they do?

Brief aside: You will want both a résumé and a completed application from each job candidate at some point prior to conducting the on-site interview(s). You will need to decide upon a process for handling this applicant-screening phase and be consistent in implementing the process. For example, in response to a job advertisement, you may receive a résumé by mail. Or, the résumé may be sent electronically. Or, you may have the capability to process online applications. Or, an applicant may need to fill out the application on-site. No matter the methodology, the process will be unique to your organization depending on the technical capabilities and setup of your process. We recommend requiring that each candidate provide you with both a résumé and a completed application prior to the phone-screen interview, which we describe below.

Biz Tip   While screening applications and résumés, don't ignore these red flags:

- Big gaps in employment
- Request not to contact prior employers
- Job-hopping (that is, moves to a new job every couple of years)
- Incomplete answers or blanks
- No references from supervisors/peers at prior employment
- Inconsistencies between information given on the résumé or the application form

PHONE-SCREEN INTERVIEW

Remember, the goal with the phone-screen interview is to identify those candidates worthy of being interviewed by the people in your organization who will have a say in selecting the right person for the job. Every conversation counts. Prepare questions beforehand and be intimately familiar with the job opening and its requirements before placing the call.

Biz Tip   While conducting the phone-screen interview, don't ignore these red flags:

- Lack of interest or enthusiasm for the opportunity
- Inconsistencies in information provided during the interview versus what's stated on the résumé or application form
- Failure to adequately answer the question, Why are you interested in this job?
- Sketchy, vague, or evasive responses

PREPARATION FOR THE ON-SITE INTERVIEW

Candidates are coming to your offices to check out their potential new place of employment. Make "the house" presentable, professional, and clean. The candidate may be waiting in your lobby for a period of time, so make that part of the experience a positive one. The reception area should be a space in which the candidate feels welcome and also learns more about the company. You know, a "trophy room" where industry accolades, positive press, and community recognition are placed front and center. (Go ahead. Walk out to the reception area right now. What kind of impression does it make?) Last, but certainly not least, the receptionist really is your "Director of First Impressions." We love that title, by the way, because it really fits what the role should be.

We started this chapter with the premise that lack of time

and/or preparation by the interviewer can undermine the effectiveness of the interview process. We've only skimmed the surface of what's required throughout the interview process, so it should be readily apparent by now that this is a very involved process when administered at full capacity. Hang on for the ride. It will be worth it.

CAREFUL ASSESSMENT AND USE OF CANDIDATE INFORMATION

Our other concern related to the art of interviewing comes with a double-edged sword. We all have massive amounts of information available to us through online access to thousands of data points: credit histories, government records, criminal activity, education and employment histories, Facebook pages, personal photos, blogs, tweets, tagged photos, and so on and so forth. This is arguably a good thing. Or is it?

With access to significant personal information about a job candidate, we must be careful about accessing and using the information. Keep in mind you can't really unwind the clock. You and your organization must plan ahead and determine how much, if any, online digging will be performed on job candidates.

We are not big fans of online data mining of job candidates. There is a risk-reward analysis that every organization must consider prior to taking this on. The most significant risk is that the organization (through HR or another decision maker in the process) may learn something about a candidate that reveals some legally protected characteristic about the individual (you know the list . . . race, color, religion, age, sex, national origin, citizenship, disability, genetic information, or other legally protected status). If the organization decides not to hire the person on the basis of a given characteristic within that list (that is, a discriminatory basis), it's clearly a problem. If you do not consider that characteristic and choose not to hire that person for a different reason, it may be difficult to prove that you really didn't use that information in making your decision. In other words, an inference could be alleged that would create the impression of a discriminatory motive.

Here's a scenario to illustrate what we mean—and to keep you up at night.

Bad Boss comes to HR and says, "I met Linda, the new candidate for the accounting representative opening, yesterday. I had my suspicions about her, so I did a Google search after the interview. Check this out."

Bad Boss drops a few pictures of Linda onto your desk. She appears to be with her girlfriend and with her daughter, who's in a wheelchair alongside a sign that says, "Walk for the Cure." They are all wearing T-shirts that say, "Linda's a survivor!"

"Yup," says Bad Boss proudly, "I knew there was something up with her. From these pictures, I'm guessing the new job candidate, Linda, is probably gay, she has a kid with problems, and her health may not be so good."

Then, in a tone of righteous indignation, Bad Boss

announces for the whole department to hear: "You know what to do. Cut her from the process now before we really have a problem on our hands."

You might as well start looking for your next "opportunity" because you're likely either going to be fired for not doing what Bad Boss asks or finding yourself in a witness chair two years from now, trying to respond to some very tough questions. Actually, maybe there is a third option: You later talk with Bad Boss, explain all the problems created by the scenario he proposed, and he backs off his directive (keep hope in your heart, HR professional).

For now, let's just agree that by doing the things we've included in the following list (sans online data mining) you have a pretty darn good chance of sufficiently screening candidates. Our recommended screening practices include:

- ☑ Conduct a relevant background check, preferably using a third-party professional.

- ☑ If you conduct a background check through a third party, have the appropriate waivers signed by the candidate (Fair Credit Reporting Act requirements).

- ☑ Be consistent among your candidates about if and when you conduct a background check, as well as the background matters to be reviewed. Carefully determine the type of background information you will seek, such as criminal record (mentioned next), driving record, credit history, etc., by considering its relevance to the job, as well as the applicable legal constraints.

☑ One caveat is to be careful about the use of criminal background information. In April 2012, the Equal Employment Opportunity Commission (EEOC) issued enforcement guidance on the use of criminal background checks that has a significant impact on access to and reliance upon criminal records as appropriate hiring criteria (*EEOC Enforcement Guidance: Consideration of Arrest & Conviction Records in Employment Decisions Under Title VII of the Civil Rights Act of 1964, 4/25/2012*). This is a rapidly changing area of the law, and you will need to carefully consider any relevant court decisions, along with the EEOC's enforcement guidance in relation to the job opening and use of criminal convictions and arrest records in a hiring decision. This is an opportunity for a quick call with your employment law counsel.

☑ Verify employment, at least the dates of employment and job titles/positions held. On these calls, we also like to ask whether the candidate is eligible for rehire; you might actually get an answer to that question.

☑ Verify education. Be sure the applicant received the degrees/certifications being claimed.

☑ Check references—always.

ON-SITE INTERVIEW(S)

Typically, in our experience, someone from HR arranges for the interview (either through his or her own efforts or through an outside recruiting source) and coordinates the logistics, such as reserving the necessary space for the interview(s), setting the interviewer(s) schedules, and preparing any material about the company to be provided to the candidate. This contact "owns" the process—or should own the process—to ensure that the interview occurs as planned. With such a level of attention to detail and expertise, how can anything possibly go wrong? Easy. Things don't go according to plan because the key ingredient in this situation is a human being, or several human beings, and we are all walking variables in any equation.

So now the candidate shows up, usually early/nervous/sweaty and in an extreme state of either chattiness or pre-interview coma. Together we are in "game time" for the interview. To say that the interview immediately starts off without incident would be naively optimistic. Either of the following situations could occur:

- The prescheduled interview room becomes unavailable because of an unplanned event, such as an impromptu employee birthday party.

- Your additional interviewers are suddenly busy, regardless of confirming their availability in response to your email/calendar reminders.

But you carry on because that is your job, and you're darn good at it. (Keep telling yourself that, it helps!) Luckily, you have done all of the following:

- Reserved a backup room (or have a default room available: your office, the office of a colleague who is out that day, etc.)

- Notified people ahead of time that they might be needed to interview and given them a general time parameter

MOJO *from* **MASTERS**

Your goals as interviewer are threefold: to keep the conversation moving along, to get answers to your questions, and to predict future behavior. That's all.

Let's look at three examples that illustrate those first two goals together. You want to keep the conversation moving forward and you want to get *your* questions answered. You are the one who's in charge.

1. If the interviewee strays from your question, it is your job to reel that person in—quickly!

> **You**: What responsibilities did you have as the manager of service at your prior employer?
>
> **Response**: Well, I certainly did more than anyone else in my area. I've never seen such a lazy group of folks in my life. I remember one weekend we were really busy with customers in a line going out the door, and I'll be darned if—
>
> **You**: Actually, I'd like to hear more about the specific duties you performed as the manager of service.
>
> **Response**: If the people in that line hadn't gotten so belligerent—
>
> **You**: Please hold that thought for right now, unless you are explaining one of your job duties.

Response: No, I just thought you might like to hear about how unruly our customers could become.

You: No, I'd prefer for you to specifically describe for me the actual duties you carried out. For example, did you answer the phone for customer complaints?

Response: Yes, I did answer the phones and respond to customer service matters, including complaints and requests for service calls.

This interviewee simply wouldn't (or couldn't) focus on your question. Once you made it clear that you didn't want to hear any more about her story, and you asked a specific question about a possible job duty, you began to get responses that were meaningful. This interviewee will likely require that kind of specific follow-up question throughout the interview.

2. If the interviewee dodges your question, ask the question as many times as necessary to get an answer. Be relentless.

You: You have indicated that you were fired from your last job. What were the circumstances that led to your firing?

Response: Well, my old boss was quite a jerk. You know the kind of guy—a routine complainer, with never anything nice to say to anyone about anything—

You: What specifically led to you being fired from that job?

Response: You know we had a few nicknames for our boss. The funniest nickname I ever heard was started by another employee—

You: Let's not get too far astray and instead focus on my question. "Why did you get fired?"

Response: That old so-and-so . . . I mean, if it wasn't one thing it was another—

You: Okay, one more time, why were you let go from your last job? I just want the specific reason for your firing.

Response: I was late to work.

You: Late or absent?

Response: Absent.

You: Just one day?

Response: No.

You: How many days?

Response: A week.

You: Did you miss an entire week?

Response: Yes.

You: Did you call in during that week?

Response: No.

You: Were you fired for missing the time or not calling in?

Response: Both.

You: Did you know that you might get fired for that?

Response: Well, yes.

It took a while, but persistence paid off. When you made it clear that dodging the question was not going to cut it, the job candidate told you what you needed to know. (And he wasn't going to answer your question otherwise.) You also pursued very specific follow-up questions that provided further information, which this candidate was certainly not going to share voluntarily.

If the interviewee goes down a path that is not responsive to your question and provides information that you really don't want to hear, stop him—dead in his tracks. You don't have to be rude, but you do want to be firm.

> **You**: Are you able to meet the requirement that the receptionist works an 8:00 a.m. to 5:00 p.m. schedule?

> **Response**: Sure. However, I have two children and am single, so I will probably run into more problems in the morning—

> **You**: Actually, I need to stop you there. I want to make it clear that I am not asking about your family situation, nor is that information relevant to my decision making. I just want to be sure you understand the job expectations. Being on time and staying to the end of the day are critical so that the front office remains properly covered.

> **Response**: Well, my children also have religious education classes on Wednesdays. We're Catholic, you see, and these classes are required—

> **You**: Stop. Again, you are giving me information that I'm not asking for, nor will I take it into consideration. My sole inquiry has to do with your ability to perform the receptionist job, which requires consistent attendance from 8:00 a.m. to 5:00 p.m. Can you perform that job duty? Just yes or no please.

> **Response**: Hmmm, I guess so.

Sound familiar? Things are never as straightforward as they should be. Your goal in such an interview is to try to get a direct answer to your question and be sure the interviewee understands that you are disregarding information that is irrelevant to your inquiry (and potentially smacks of discrimination).

NOTE: Don't write down those potentially discriminatory-sounding remarks in your interview notes. You aren't going to base your decision on the applicant's gender, religion, or any other protected status. So don't allow the notes to look like it.

The third goal in this trifecta is to predict future behavior based on responses in the interview. (Shoot, where is that crystal ball when you really need it?) An extremely popular method for posing such questions is the behavioral interviewing technique in which the interviewer asks questions about a candidate's past actions to predict how the candidate will behave in the future.

Biz Tip   We have provided a few examples of behavioral questions:

1. Give an example of a goal you achieved and the steps you took to reach that goal.
2. Tell about a time when you faced a difficult work situation and how you handled it.
3. Have you ever made a mistake at work? How did you handle it?
4. Describe a decision you made that was unpopular and how you handled making that decision, as well as implementing it.

Tactics: Where do I go from here?

It's time to create the best and most *effective* (there's that word again) interview process that can work in most industries and for most positions, allowing for any editing or modifying as you may need.

Beginning with the end in mind, throughout the interview process remind yourself that you are trying to find the candidate who:

1. Best fits the job criteria based on the listed responsibilities, tasks required, experience, and education

2. Integrates well into the existing culture and with the staff

3. Displays important qualities such as initiative, intelligence, adaptability, and honesty, along with strong communication skills

Yes, this would describe the perfect candidate, and yes, perfect (or near-perfect) candidates do exist. Remember, the effective interview is much more than merely asking the questions on a page. This is an opportunity to interact with a job candidate and learn more than can be gleaned from a résumé and a cover letter. This interview is important to the candidate; it should be equally important to the interviewer. Having refined this through trial and error, here is our version of the most effective interview process to implement in your workplace.

PRE-INTERVIEW PREPARATION

Be sure you've done your homework. Know the answers to the following questions well before the first job candidate ever steps foot on company soil for an interview:

- What is the job?

- Is it a replacement or new job?

- If it's a new job, where does it go on the organizational chart?

- If it's a replacement, does the business need an exact replacement or a different set of skills?

- What is the proper market compensation for the position?

- Is the job description accurate?

- Who needs to be involved in the interviewing?

- Who needs to be involved in the selection decision?

- What is the time frame for filling the position?

INTERVIEW QUESTIONS

Prepare questions in advance that not only address the skills required for the position but are also geared toward the candidate's own education and work history. Again, do your homework. By knowing the candidate's background, you are ready to ask appropriate follow-up questions with ease.

Be sure the questions elicit information that will be helpful in assessing each candidate's experience in relation to the job as well as the candidate's ability to truly perform the required duties.

Take the job description and formulate questions related to each of the written duties, tasks, and responsibilities. Also develop questions that will extract responses that provide a glimpse into the future. In other words, behavioral questioning (as described on page 40) that is relevant to the job and the candidate. Be consistent from candidate to candidate with the questions you ask to avoid bias or the appearance of bias in the process.

MOJO *from* MASTERS

If different interview questions are asked among job candidates or questions are asked that otherwise seem based on protected status, an opening may be created for an assertion of discrimination. When the same questions are not asked consistently, or potentially biased questions are asked, it may appear that the questions are being asked to accomplish a subtle, discriminatory purpose. If a certain question is missing from one interview it could lead a skeptic to believe the interviewer had intentionally left out the question to "skip" a potentially good answer from the candidate. Conversely, the skeptic might suggest that a certain question was "added" in order to create a tougher interview for another candidate. Interviewers should ask questions consistently in order to avoid such insinuations. Interviewers also should not ask questions related to protected status to avoid any inference of discriminatory bias being asserted.

INTERVIEW LOGISTICS

Ensure that the interview room is an appropriate private setting in which to have a conversation. Allow enough time to have a comfortable dialogue that doesn't feel rushed. This is critical, particularly if you want to create a positive impression with the candidate. An interview that is rushed may make the candidate feel like an afterthought or simply not a priority—neither of which is good.

In addition, make sure the interviewing and hiring process is explained in advance to the candidate, creating the proper expectations for all involved. If the interview involves multiple conversations throughout several hours to a full day, an agenda can be a valuable tool to give to a job candidate. First, this sets the expectation for how long each interview will last. Be sure to include each interviewer's title and department on the agenda. The candidate will also have a source to later refer to for contact information, spelling of names, job titles, etc., which facilitates the candidates' follow-up should they have further questions.

THE INTERVIEW

It sounds cliché, but this moment of meeting the candidate is a first impression for both of you. Welcome and greet the candidate in a friendly manner, making her feel comfortable in the interview room. Reiterate details about the interviewing and hiring processes at your company.

Focus on questions that are job specific and relevant to this open position, allowing for discussion from the candidate. Avoid those questions that give the candidate the opportunity to give one-word answers: You want discussion, not brief answers.

Don't allow the candidate to answer questions using "we" or "they" when describing group tasks; you want to know specifically what the candidate did in a particular situation. Encourage questions from the candidate about how they see their goals being met in your organization, how they see themselves contributing to your company, and any other work-related topic. End the interview with a brief recap of the process.

Biz Tip   Here's a practice pointer about interview notes.

- Don't write on the résumé or application itself. (Have a clean sheet of paper or notebook in which to record each interview.)
- Keep separate written notes from each interview.
- Document the responses carefully and as verbatim as possible.
- Do not write "reminders" to yourself that could be misconstrued as discriminatory comments (i.e., blonde, young, old, glasses, skinny, fat, gray hair, limp, Asian-looking, black, Jewish, etc.). In other words, no shorthand notes about characteristics that in any way relate to a protected category.
- Retain all interview notes from each interview. (Store interview documentation by position in a locked file cabinet.)

POST-INTERVIEW COMMUNICATION

After you've reviewed all of the interviewed candidates' information and made your selection (and the "selectee" accepts), communicate the outcome in a letter to the balance of the candidates who participated in the process by thanking them for their interest in your company.

BOTTOM LINE

As we previously stated, one reason why we consider interviewing a lost art starts with the premise that effective interviews take time—and we simply don't have it. It takes time to screen résumés, make yes and no piles, conduct phone interviews, make further selection decisions, contact those selected for interviews, handle the interview setup/logistics, prepare interview questions relevant to the job and candidate, conduct the interviews, evaluate the candidates, make more selection decisions, make the job offer, wait for a response, and contact those candidates who were not selected. Whew!

The second reason we think interviewing is a lost art is that the modern-day interviewer has other avenues through which to gather information about the candidates. This allows the interviewer to rely less on the interview itself and more on other techniques of data mining.

The reality, however, is that now more than ever we must make time to interview correctly; it is too critical to the ongoing success of the business. When we do our homework, use our best predictive questions, and determine that our job opening is in alignment with a particular applicant's skill set, we can make the perfect hire (or at least come pretty darn close). Take the time. Interview with intentionality. You'll be so glad you did.

CHAPTER 3

It's Time to Seal the Deal

SURPRISE! THE WELCOMING COMMITTEE IS ON VACATION

I have not failed. I've just found 10,000 ways that won't work.
—Thomas A. Edison

There are two key functions in the hiring phase of the employee life cycle we want to cover in this chapter: job offers (seal the deal, baby) and onboarding (the welcome wagon). These functions are interrelated with the recruiting and interviewing functions because the job candidate—soon to be new employee—will be interested in knowing whether everything discussed up to this point is going to come true (enter glass slipper and carriage). This is a very critical time for the employee, who will either become an instant cheerleader or will be asking, "Is this what they call a bait and switch?"

Your people have likely spent time talking to the candidate about the awesome corporate culture and business reputation of the organization. The next way in which that *awesomeness* will be tested is how well the job offer is communicated. This is also known as the "Ask." You might remember high schoolers spending countless hours determining how to cleverly "ask" a date to homecoming or the prom, using techniques from messages delivered in pizza boxes to airplane skywriting. The Ask is all about delivering a request (using memorable tactics) to be sure the reply is yes. If job offers received half the amount of attention that the Ask receives, there would be an astonishing increase in job-offer acceptance rates.

Equally critical, after the Ask (um . . . job offer) is delivered and accepted, the first day, week, month on the job ensues. We must have a well-defined plan in place to ensure that our first impression out of the gate makes a positive, lasting impression. It is important that the candidate continues to see consistency between the organization's words and actions.

Tales: Am I the only sane person in the room?

One of the most memorable job offers ever delivered involved an offer from a law firm to a graduating newbie law student (you have to guess which one of us). The recruiting partners were a fun-loving, charismatic duo (and, yes, they were lawyers). As part of their effort to impress this very impressionable law school grad, they not only communicated a very nice offer to become a first-year associate attorney with their law firm but also drove to the student's apartment to personally deliver the offer. As if that weren't enough, the recruiting duo also left behind a new, shiny convertible Mustang for this student to drive during the next week while considering their job offer. (One of the partners had a family member who owned an auto dealership, which gave him ready access to vehicles.) The car was on loan for just a week, but the lasting impression ensued.

Let's compare that tale to another communication of a job offer in which the applicant was contacted, about a week after the interview, by a company representative with whom the applicant had never spoken. The conversation began with the representative calling the applicant by the wrong first name (confusion over a nickname that had been clarified during the interview). No apology ensued, just a lame excuse. The blunders continued as the job offer was made for the wrong job. Really. The company was hiring like crazy, and they couldn't keep the pace. The paperwork had been so bungled that similar mistakes occurred two more times before the day ended. Unfortunately in this situation, a lasting impression was also created.

How about a quick tale regarding the first day on the job at two different companies? At the first company (Good Boss's company), the new employee was greeted with a welcome packet from the receptionist upon arrival. She was then given a tour of the building and introduced to coworkers. There was a nameplate in her office, along with business cards and fully stocked office supplies. Several department colleagues took her out to lunch, and the afternoon included a presentation that covered everything but the kitchen sink regarding the company.

The other new hire (at Bad Boss's company) was greeted by a receptionist who had no clue about his arrival. He was left in the reception area for the first thirty minutes without any explanation. When he was finally shown to an office, which appeared to have been quickly abandoned by the last occupant, he was given a stack of company documents to read on his own while HR tried to find something for him to do that afternoon. Need we say more?

Tips: What else do I need to know?

There are so many variables to the offer, hiring, and onboarding game that it can be difficult to ensure complete success every time. However, this is an area where, when done right, you can win people over from the start, and it will ultimately have a positive, lasting impression.

SEAL THE DEAL: MAKING THE JOB OFFER AND GETTING AN ACCEPTANCE

The first question is, who is going to place the call and make the offer of employment? Typically, the hiring manager or other member of management with whom the candidate has spoken makes the offer. HR is also often called upon to make the offer or to be present in the conversation. Not always, but 99.9 percent of the time, a job offer is first verbally communicated. Then a written offer letter is sent as a follow-up to the conversation. The letter is also an important document because it is often the only written source that clarifies terms of an offer after memories have gone fuzzy.

With regard to the verbal job offer, know the terms and state them clearly. Be enthusiastic. Handling the "Ask" is actually one of the fun parts of your job. Be prepared with information including the job title, start date, name of the direct supervisor, compensation, pre-employment testing (if required), an offer expiration date, as well as the location of the job if there are multiple job sites. Be prepared for questions about benefits, vacation, holidays, and other employment policy questions that relate to the particular job. You certainly don't have to offer a sporty loaner car or go to other extreme measures to make a solid offer of employment.

SEAL THE DEAL: GETTING THE NEW EMPLOYMENT RELATIONSHIP OFF TO A GOOD START

Let's move to the first day of employment, often referred to as onboarding. The format of one's first day of employment may either be specific to the one new hire or be created for a broader audience of new hires. The new-employee orientation, whether on a large or small scale, can either be informative and even enjoyable or pure blunt head trauma for all parties involved.

The new hire always has paperwork to complete and copy machine training to endure. Some things are hard to avoid. But what happens next is where it gets interesting. Does the brand-new employee then go to her desk and fend for herself? Would an organization really leave a new employee parked at her desk for six hours without any interaction from her supervisor and colleagues on her first day? Yes, it happens, and it results in a first-impression moment lost. We won't settle for that.

Tactics: Where do I go from here?

Let's start with the tactics for the offer. The offer letter is a reiteration of everything that was stated in the verbal job offer (which typically comes first). An offer letter often has a signature line for the job candidate, who is required to countersign the letter as an acknowledgment of accepting the offer and the employment terms stated in the letter.

Biz Tip   Key elements of an offer letter:

- Job title
- Start date
- Supervisor's name
- Compensation
- Pre-employment testing, if required
- An expiration date for the offer

Make extending the offer a simple and painless process. It can be hard to find the right hire, and you've worked like a dog to get this far. Let's get that person successfully through the hiring gauntlet; there is no reason to punish them with a poorly communicated "Do you want the job or not?" sentiment. After the verbal conversation, prepare and send a well-written, clearly stated offer letter that includes the elements stated above.

If you are making a conditional job offer, meaning that the offer is not fully effectuated until certain conditions are met, you must be extremely precise and clear. A conditional job offer, for example, might require that the offeree successfully pass a drug test or physical examination. If the offeree doesn't pass, the offer is withdrawn.

Be aware that certain post-offer, pre-employment testing is subject to scrutiny under applicable laws, such as the Americans with Disabilities Act Amendments Act (ADAAA). We could fill the pages of another book exclusively about litigation, regulations, legislative guidance, and real-life drama on that topic. Since we can't do it justice here, suffice it to say that this is a topic which requires careful consideration on a case-by-case basis when you're on the front lines (and likely warrants another call to your favorite employment lawyer).

Another important element of the offer relates to non-compete agreements. When applicable, there are two key considerations. The first is the fact that you may require the new hire to sign a non-compete as a condition of employment. The second is that you may require the new hire to affirm in writing that he or she is not in violation of some other non-compete agreement before accepting employment with your company.

A final element of the job offer is communicating when an offer expires. Typically, an offer is extended with the expectation that it will remain open for consideration by the candidate for a period of days. Usually, the time frame is about a week. Certain positions, such as key or uniquely qualified hires, may be given a longer time for consideration. The main point here is that we don't want to hold ourselves hostage to an outstanding offer for too long. Yet, we also don't want to mistakenly think an offeree has taken the outsanding offer off the table, offer the job to a second applicant who accepts, only to have the first candidate accept thereafter.

THE WELCOME WAGON HAS ARRIVED: HOW TO MAKE A LASTING IMPRESSION ON THE FIRST DAY

Looks like the courtship is over and the candidate is yours! What does the first day/week/month look like for the new employee? Why does it matter? Again, these are critical moments of truth for the newbie. Engage the new employee early on. Regardless of his level of experience in the workplace, he is new to *your* company and this is your chance to really make this the beginning of an extraordinary employee experience. On the first day, make your new employee feel like he made the right choice.

Biz Tip Two golden rules for the first day:

- Don't (ever) leave the new employee alone on the first day for long periods of time. (Recall from experience, on the first day, even short time frames seem long.)
- Be sure the new employee has someone to eat lunch with!

You will want to create a strong impression and cover the basics on the new employee's first day. You will need to make your approach fit your corporate culture. Remember, this is the new employee's first experience of your company's culture and your goal should be to help the employee form a positive, lasting impression. In your own unique way, you will want to cover as many of the items on the following checklist as possible, adding your own as necessary.

- ☑ Tour of building and location of important areas (e.g., restrooms, break room)

- ☑ Introductions (usually while on the tour)

- ☑ Employee handbook (discuss selected provisions)

- ☑ Benefits and related forms to fill out

- ☑ New-hire paperwork to fill out (e.g., I-9, tax forms, contact information)

- ☑ Equipment (e.g., key card, computer, cell phone)

- ☑ Building access and parking

- ☑ Business cards, if applicable

- ☑ Office phone number and email address

BOTTOM LINE

Let's say it together: "You never get a second chance to make a first impression." Our opportunity to start off on the right foot with a new hire begins at the job offer and is carried throughout those first days of employment. Take the time to evaluate your current way of doing things. Ask yourself how impressed you would be as a new hire at your company. If you aren't satisfied with your answer, walk through each of the steps above to create a new way of doing things. You'll create an impression that will have lasting value. You'll be so glad you did.

Part II

BABYSITTER: NURTURE AND GUIDE

A babysitter is responsible for keeping a close eye on his or her charges, along with giving direction and watching closely for behaviors to be rewarded or scolded. Similarly, a manager keeps a close eye on his or her charges by engaging in HR functions such as performance reviews, employee retention and development strategies, and employee reward programs to provide guidance in the workplace.

CHAPTER 4

False Hope, Faint Praise & the Unintended Consequences of the Performance Appraisal

I always wanted to be somebody, but now
I realize I should have been a little more specific.
—Lily Tomlin

The term "performance management" is really an oxymoron. Rarely, if ever, does a manager truly *manage* an employee's performance. Oftentimes, a manager waits until the employee or the department is in crisis before addressing any performance deficiencies. Over the years, it has been our experience that meaningful discussions or feedback about an individual's performance usually come too late or not at all. From the HR perspective (c'mon, back us up on this), we have seen appraisal forms that appear to be simply copied from the previous year or, even better, completed by the employee and signed by the manager. A true performance evaluation that the supervisor put a lot of thought into? Nope. An assessment of skills and abilities utilized by the employee over the past year? Not so much. An opportunity to create an action plan or set performance goals? Still nothin'.

For example, consider the employee who would cringe every time her manager asked for a copy of last year's appraisal a week before the next appraisal was due—and then would await receipt of a remarkably similar review. What a waste of time, money, and energy, not to mention a real credibility killer for the organization.

Why does this happen? Because performance management may require the deliverer to have a difficult conversation, address performance deficiencies, or otherwise bring up tough issues in the discussion.

We get it. Having a conversation about great job performance is relatively easy—and certainly painless. The opposite also holds true. Having a conversation about poor job performance can be difficult—and sometimes painful. Ergo, the last thing most people seek out is a discussion in which they are going to call out deficiencies in another person.

Not all managers loathe the performance appraisal process, though. Some of them love this chance to provide feedback. Admittedly, the task is far more pleasant when the feedback is positive, but even in a difficult evaluation, by using an honest, information-laden process, the manager can truly address areas that are working, areas that have improved, areas that still need work, and an action plan on how to close any gaps in performance. When perfectly executed, the performance review is a thing of HR beauty, especially when the appraisal actually moves the employee's performance forward in a positive manner.

There are so many elements to performance management, and the appraisal is just one of them. As we've seen, the performance appraisal process can be easily derailed, creating even further problems for the organization. Preparation and training are needed to do it right—in other words, handle with care. Training your managers on how to create, deliver, and fully execute performance management processes would surely result in better productivity and higher employee satisfaction.

Tales: Am I the only sane person in the room?

In the array of responsibilities required for implementation of a performance management process, the responsible party (an HR representative, the direct supervisor, or someone from upper management) will need to administer the nuts and bolts of the process, as well as work toward effective outcomes with both successful and unsuccessful employees to the point of promotion or employment termination. This is (should be) an ongoing and fluid task that occurs consistently throughout an employee's tenure.

But what about the situation in which none of those duties are being performed? That is, if HR, direct supervisors, and upper management are nowhere to be found? We have witnessed too many circumstances where performance management is nonexistent until a real crisis is about to strike. Here's how it shakes out.

The employee, let's call her Laurie, is a poor performer and has been for a long time. But she tries hard, and her heart is in the right place, so time marches on with her marginal performance never being addressed. Department Manager begins a closer analysis of the output in the department and decides that Laurie just isn't hitting the mark. Department Manager tells Direct Supervisor, "Look, I know it won't be easy, but you're going to have to do something about Laurie." Within the blink of an eye—and right before Laurie is handed either a performance warning or notice of job termination—voilà! Laurie moves in with a beautifully timed preemptive strike and lodges a separate, unrelated complaint about her direct supervisor prior to the corrective action. How did Laurie know what was coming? We have no idea. What we do know is that the absence of any prior performance reviews or documentation about missed goals, missed deadlines, failed performance, etc., will not be helpful to the company's current position that Laurie's performance was poor and requires corrective action. The timing of Laurie's complaint makes it more difficult for the company to move forward with its plan to (finally) address her job performance deficiencies.

In such situations, an employee may assert a complaint about a decision-maker (department manager, supervisor, etc.). Yes, the very same people who are likely putting the final touches on the employee's discharge paperwork or other disciplinary matter. The complaint is typically about something that the individual said or did that is just dicey enough that it can't be ignored. Now the dilemma is whether to move forward with the impending negative performance-related action or to put it on hold for fear that a retaliation claim will surely follow.

Generally speaking, retaliation occurs when an employer takes an adverse action against a covered individual because he/she engaged in a "protected activity." Protected activity includes action by an employee such as raising a complaint about inappropriate (harassing) conduct in the workplace.

Let's look at a slight variation of this. Another employee, whom we'll call Larry, had been working under a "final" ninety-day warning for unsatisfactory performance, and he was nearing the end of the ninety days. In this situation, the company had been carrying out its performance management process. About Day 80 of the probation for poor performance, Larry reported to Plant Manager that his supervisor had been bullying him. Larry added that the behavior has been going on for a long time, but recently it had become more intolera- ble. (NOTE: Plant Manager must think strategically from the start. In fact, this is one of the most critical junctures as events unfold. Unfortunately, Plant Manager wasn't interested in such thinking. But we'll get back to that.) Plant Manager was immediately dismissive of Larry and believed his complaint was nothing more than a last-ditch effort to avoid finishing out the day. Larry happened to be working on a machine that day that sorely tested his skills. Plant Manager told him to go back to work and "quit his whining." Larry refused, and said that he'd put up with his supervisor's bullying long enough and couldn't take it anymore. Plant Manager was not about to back down at this point. He told Larry to get back to his machine or he was fired. Larry refused and he was handed his walking papers.

Yes, we are still talking performance management. Interestingly, this tale teaches us that implementation of the performance management process can have far-reaching implications.

The next communication from Larry was an EEOC charge in which he alleged that he had been subjected to wrongful termination, harassment, and retaliation. For the first time, the company learned from the allegations in the charge that the supervisor in Larry's area was routinely referring to the guys in the department as "meatheads" and "boy-toys." The supervisor often asked the male employees to discuss their sexual preference, to give him an update on their weekend "escapades," and to regularly pledge a vow to their "manliness." Later, other male employees—who had brushed off their supervisor as offensive, but half crazy—affirmed these allegations. (NOTE: When asked why they hadn't previously reported their supervisor, the men responded that the Plant Manager wouldn't have done anything anyway since he and the Direct Supervisor were buddies.) The Direct Supervisor also made it very clear that anyone who challenged him would join the unemployment line.

Several moments of truth here indicate a failure in the handling of the performance management process. One critical juncture was the assumption by Plant Manager that Larry was attempting to derail the performance-related probation at the eleventh hour by raising a "red-herring" complaint. As such, Plant Manager failed to address Larry's complaint. Worse still, as a buddy of Direct Supervisor, the Plant Manager may simply have seen this as an opportunity to pull the trigger and help his buddy along the way.

The point is we should never, ever make assumptions. Our job is to stay the course in implementing whatever program is in place, while handling the unexpected divergence (employee complaint) on a parallel track. In this example, the better course would have been to follow the performance management process (by continuing down the final warning path) while exercising consistency and keen judgment throughout every step—without moving straight to a job termination under those circumstances. A key moment occurred when Larry complained. It was a strategic point in time when a different approach could have made all the difference. Plant Manager should not have assumed that Larry's complaint was a preemptive strike, nor should he have immediately fired Larry under those circumstances. Plant Manager should have initiated an investigation, and he might have uncovered what Larry meant by "bullying." At least by looking into the allegation, the company would have had the opportunity to determine the legitimacy of the concern. Instead, the failure to take the complaint seriously and the lack of follow-up into the complaint—along with the firing—walked the company straight into treacherous territory.

The integrity of the performance management process could also have been maintained if the company had launched an investigation. Although extreme care would need to be exercised (probably time to speed dial the company's employment lawyer), the company might have been able to continue to address both the complaint and the employee's performance issues at the same time on two separate yet parallel tracks.

MOJO *from* MASTERS

- Meaningful performance management processes enhance communication channels and help management understand potential issues before they spin out of control. Oftentimes, through the course of performance discussions and providing feedback, employers uncover critical information from the employee ranks.

- Performance management is the overarching process by which management sets expectations for employee performance—and measures the employee's ability to meet those expectations. The process requires attention and consistency—or matters become overlooked until calamity strikes.

- Companies must make it clear to employees and managers that complaints will be taken seriously. Management must consistently and effectively respond to and handle complaints as part of the overall process.

- Meaningful training for supervisors must emphasize three key goals: the supervisor's own behavior must be appropriate; the supervisor must address all complaints; and, the supervisor must constantly be objective in workplace dealings.

Tips: What else do I need to know?

There are five key elements to consider for a successful performance-management program.

1. Performance goals and criteria development.

2. Job descriptions and performance appraisals.

3. Documentation.

4. Delivering performance feedback.

5. Training on performance management.

We are going to discuss each of these in the Tactics section, but first we want to focus on two common themes we've seen throughout our careers, both of which impact the success of any performance-management system. The first is lack of communication about performance 364 out of 365 days of the year. The second is avoidance of the difficult conversations with poor performers, which we touched on at the start of this chapter.

True performance management does not wait until the annual review; rather, performance management should be an active and ongoing two-way dialogue. Not top-down, not paint-by-numbers, and definitely not one-size-fits-all. The performance discussions that happen as part of one's daily interactions deliver the greatest value. The caution is to not allow the annual performance-review discussion to suffer from either the "recency effect" or the "trash-compactor syndrome."

The recency effect simply refers to the problem that, in an annual review, we may forget the prior eleven months of the review period and simply focus on only the most recent events. When this happens, the employees will not receive complete feedback about their full performance for the year, and they may be subject to an inflated review—one way or the other, either positive or negative—depending on how the past month has gone.

The trash-compactor syndrome relates to the fact that when performance feedback is provided at only one time during the year, the reviewer will have "held" onto information for a long time and will then spew it out all at once like an erupting volcano. Not only will the employee be overwhelmed by the amount of information; the employee may also have lost opportunities throughout the prior year to work on the matter if it was an area requiring improvement.

The good news here is we have an easy fix: Talk more, and often. Remember the TV commercial AT&T ran in which the adult moderator sits at a table with young children and asks, "Which is better—more or less?" The resounding reply was, "More is better . . . we want more, more." We need to get in the habit of talking more, and on a routine basis, with employees about their performance—both the good and the bad—so that there are no surprises on annual review day. The communication (feedback) should be conversational, not formal. Over time it will become engrained in your company's culture.

Biz Tip   Talk more, and often!

With regard to our human tendency to avoid difficult conversations, performance management becomes either Judgment Day or Christmas Day. If we've been holding difficult information for a year, waiting for (and dreading) the annual review, it's not Christmas. If it helps, we've never met anyone who looks forward to the difficult conversations. Here's how you can help yourself in these situations:

- **Get on the issue early**. Waiting only prolongs the pain. Consider that it's like a Band-Aid: one quick yank and it's over. The more timely and routine the feedback, there is a greater likelihood that the performance problem can be nipped in the bud. Keep in mind that you're evaluating the person's job performance, not the person. You can validate the person ("I appreciate that you are trying hard . . .") while also identifying that their performance is not meeting your expectations (". . . however, you are not keeping up with the production needs of the department").

- **Be candid**. This is the toughest part. However, keep in mind that you are actually doing the employee a favor by identifying performance deficiencies so she can address the issue and hopefully improve. If the employee is never told about existing performance problems, she will not have the opportunity to fix them.

Tactics: Where do I go from here?

An effective performance management process is a targeted approach to evaluate and develop the company's primary assets—its employees. It is beyond argument that such an investment in the employee base can result in lower turnover, higher employee satisfaction, higher productivity, and in the end, an increased bottom line for the business. Let's delve into the five key elements for developing or improving your company's performance management program.

PERFORMANCE GOALS & CRITERIA DEVELOPMENT

Each employee needs defined expectations for achievement, growth, and contribution. Communicated goals provide a pathway for a more equitable way of evaluating individual performance. The established goals may also address areas of need and guide career development, and they should align the employee with the company's overall goals. The individual goals should each have an action plan, meet specific criteria, be objective and measurable, and be written in clear terms, as well as be challenging but achievable. What follows is an example of how this all comes together.

Performance Goal Development

List a corporate goal, and identify personal and/or department goals that align with the corporate goal and are measurable and specific:

1. **Corporate Goal**: Increase customer satisfaction in the US domestic market from current 30 percent overall satisfactory rating to 75 percent overall satisfactory rating in the next year.

2. **Personal Goals:** Customer Service Representative

   a. **Goal #1:** Resolve customer complaints within twenty-four hours. Track calls and response times to be reviewed with manager on monthly basis.

b. **Goal #2:** Create a customer survey form to obtain customer feedback by the end of Q1.

c. **Goal #3:** Track customer survey responses starting Q2. Create a report on the responses and review monthly with manager to evaluate specific areas of customer satisfaction/dissatisfaction.

Biz Tip   A performance goal that is simply stated as "improve customer satisfaction" is a road to nowhere. Employees must have specific targets (either work-product goals, due dates, and/or quantifiable objectives) in order to make actual progress and to measure the results.

JOB DESCRIPTIONS & PERFORMANCE APPRAISALS

Clear and targeted job descriptions can serve as the foundation for performance appraisals. By connecting the required tasks and accountabilities for the employee to the appraisal document, the manager is in a better position to assess performance, to identify positive and negative areas, and to openly discuss future opportunities.

The performance appraisal must also be carefully crafted to ensure that it is measuring individual performance in line with the company's business goals and strategy. For example, if the company places particular importance on conducting business in an ethical manner, then the performance appraisal should include criteria upon which to measure an employee's conduct in relation to ethical business practices.

The measurable criteria on the performance appraisal form could be stated as follows:

- Employee has a working knowledge of the ethical standards and compliance requirements associated with the job and exercises sound business judgment in fulfilling those responsibilities; or,

- Employee demonstrates personal accountability in performing duties by taking responsibility for business matters within his or her control and engaging in decision making that is based upon applicable ethical and legal standards.

DOCUMENTATION

Written documentation is valuable for two reasons. First, the process is tracking performance and communication between management and employee for development purposes. This is a pro-active and business-related purpose. Second, this same tracking or capturing of performance expectations and measurement of the related performance on a contemporaneous basis may ultimately serve as an important paper trail should the company ever need to defend its actions or explain certain employment decisions, such as a decision not to promote or a decision to fire an employee. The written documentation underlying any such decision must be prepared with a high degree of accuracy and careful attention.

The classic example of deficient documentation typically involves a less-than-stellar employee who is on the verge of being fired for poor job performance. Upon further review of the employee's potential job termination for poor performance, it is discovered that the employee has consistently received the highest rating (4's and 5's on a 5-point scale) on all performance criteria on prior years' written performance appraisals. The employer's dilemma is that the employee likely has no idea that she's been underperforming for all those years, since no one had the "hard" conversation, and, even worse, the company's own records show the employee has been a top performer. If asked, many well-intentioned managers would admit that they've been more positive or glowing about an employee's performance than was actually warranted by the employee's performance. This is a tough pill to swallow for the manager who now has to get this situation back on track.

Another potential hazard relates to the content of the written comments on the performance appraisal forms. Although they render a similar outcome, different problems can arise simply as a result of poorly chosen words. Review the following performance appraisal excerpts and see what you think:

- The written performance appraisal says, "Employee lacks the right corporate image by choosing to wear pants, instead of skirts, and leaning toward a masculine style that lacks femininity, poise, and grace." The word choice conjures up inferences of sex stereotyping and gender discrimination.

- The written performance appraisal says, "Employee fails to be a team player when it comes to tolerating coworker banter and allowing light-hearted jokes and teasing among our team." These words leave the reader guessing. The undefined terms "banter," "jokes," and "teasing" are, without further explanation, problematic.

Is the manager actually referencing behavior that may constitute harassment? Or is the manager subtly creating a chilling effect to ensure that the employee never comes forward with a complaint?

After the written performance appraisals are completed, it is wise to have them reviewed by an HR representative who proofreads the written comments to be sure that the feedback is clear and concise, not vague or ambiguous. As you select a "reviewer," keep in mind that the person should have a strong understanding of employment laws and an understanding of the confidentiality obligations related to the material being reviewed. It will be tempting to skip this step. Don't.

DELIVERING PERFORMANCE FEEDBACK

There is a right way and a very wrong way to deliver performance feedback. The place, the time, the messaging, and your specific delivery are all factors in play. As with other one-on-one meetings, the manager should prepare in advance for the meeting, especially if the news will be difficult or disheartening for the employee. This is a meeting that is expected to be a two-way dialogue, so the manager or HR representative or whoever is administering the appraisal should be prepared to address concerns or issues that may be raised by the employee. Also, this is an opportunity to work with the employee to identify goals and action plans. It pays to be a good listener during performance appraisal meetings and conversations since it's also an opportune time for managers to informally survey employees.

PROVIDE TRAINING

A final critical part of performance management is to train the management staff member who is responsible for delivering and administering the program. To be successful, the implementation of the process must be done well. And, as we've noted, many of these tasks do not come easily.

Biz Tip Important elements to cover in performance management training:

- Provide words and phrases that can be starters for the written appraisal content.
- Explain the performance criteria and the ratings so that managers provide an accurate performance assessment.
- Use role-playing so that managers can "practice" having difficult conversations.
- Work with managers to set the expectation that their role is to provide feedback on job performance to aid the employee in identifying strengths and weaknesses.
- Remind managers that an employee has the chance to "fix" something only if it's been identified.
- Recommend strategies for managers to maintain notes throughout the year so that they have specific examples of performance (good or bad) to include in the appraisal.

In light of all the responsibilities carried out by a manager, it can be tough to get them on board for one more task, especially one as difficult as performance management. We need to focus less on the administrative tasks and more on the importance of the task to the employee and the organization.

BOTTOM LINE

The bottom line is simple. Failing to effectively manage the performance of the company's employees is akin to corporate suicide. So don't fail. Implement programs that are an investment in the employees, which ultimately equate to an investment in the sustainability of the business itself. Create a system that evaluates an employee's performance in relation to measurable performance goals. Regularly communicate with the employee and provide feedback on performance, both positive and not so positive. Be sure that the performance goals set for the employee are aligned with the organization's goals. And, finally, don't put off until tomorrow what you can do today. Have the difficult conversations when required, and provide praise when merited. You'll be so glad you did.

CHAPTER 5

Fool's Gold & Free Coffee

EMPLOYEE RETENTION AT ITS FINEST

I am convinced that nothing we do
is more important than hiring and developing people.
At the end of the day you bet on people, not on strategies.

—Larry Bossidy

Let's face it: To be successful and sustainable, your business needs to retain its talented performers. It's all about keeping the right people around, and it will take more than fool's gold and free coffee to make this happen. Start with the premise that doing *something* is better than doing *nothing*. For lasting success, we need to be sure that your something is working. And to retain the best and brightest, your something needs to be more than just a paycheck.

Your something can include any one or more of the following employee retention tools: employee development plans, continuing education and/or professional development courses, succession planning, mentoring, multidisciplinary rotations, executive coaching, team-building, and career paths.

It sounds simple enough, but this area is often slighted. Considered too expensive, too time-consuming, or too illusive in terms of a company's return on investment, employee retention programs are sometimes relegated to a back room where the employees may have access to self-teaching tools or professional development courses taught by a wayward sage of the company. Not all companies feel this way, but the issue is prevalent enough that we recommend you dedicate the next half hour to reading this chapter.

Tales: Am I the only sane person in the room?

Many factors come into play when you're trying to assist an employee in his career progression and to achieve your goal of employee retention. Whether it's an employee development program, a succession plan, or a mentoring program that is a part of your organization's employee retention strategy, you are headed in the right direction if you're already using some of these strategies. However, let's look even deeper. Part of getting this right is not only determining the best employee retention tools for your business but also determining if you are implementing the program with properly trained, sufficiently equipped personnel.

Our starting point is Good Boss's business, which has developed an Employee Development Plan and is actively using it. For the sake of argument, let's also assume that the program is well-defined and well-communicated and contains meaningful and achievable expectations. Through this process the managers are readily identifying key employees and working with them on an individual basis to determine job skills to be worked on and ways to improve both their personal aptitudes and professional proficiences. Once the list has been created, the real work begins. Employees are scheduled to meet quarterly to review any outstanding action items or deliverables within their development plans and to assess any need for further work to guarantee success. In other words, at those quarterly meetings, the employee and the manager have a conversation during which they identify mutually beneficial outcomes. When this happens on a consistent basis, Good Boss can breathe a little easier, knowing there is meaningful, ongoing dialogue through which employee performance and development are being measured and improved.

Let's check in with Bad Boss, who also understands the importance of employee retention and has undertaken efforts to create Employee Development Plans for key employees. Unfortunately, Bad Boss has mostly unskilled, undisciplined, or simply careless managers. Most importantly, Bad Boss assumes his managers should know how to do this. Consequently, there's been little to no communication about the plans or any training about how to implement the program.

Without the requisite understanding of the how-tos, the program is sabotaged from the start.

Without any training or direction, the likelihood of success is diminished and a renegade manager may ruin the outcome. The following are types of managers who implement Bad Boss's program.

A WOLF IN SHEEP'S CLOTHING

This type of manager botches it by allowing self-serving motives to overrun the purpose of the program. He over-delegates responsibilities to employees under the guise of training and development. This is a great way to get others to do your work for you. The manager sets goals for employees that actually accomplish his own tasks. At the end of the day, the employees may have learned how to complete a given task but perhaps that task is not necessarily for their own betterment.

GLENDA, THE GOOD WITCH

This manager doesn't want to create any waves, avoids conflict at all costs (including her own credibility), and wants to please everyone—the employee, her own supervisor, and upper-level management. In this manager's world, everyone is a winner. Action plans are written so that goals are easily achieved. No one really wins (other than, arguably, the employee for a short time). Under this manager, the employee becomes stagnant. The employee hasn't been challenged, the manager isn't truly managing, and the employee's performance is likely falling short of the organizational goals.

MONKEY SEE, MONKEY DO

This manager creates Employee Development Plans exactly as his fellow managers do, without regard to the individual skill sets or experience of his subordinates. Remember, when done correctly, this is not a one-size-fits-all process. A slight variation on this management style is use of the "same as last year" template for an employee's current year plan—requiring zero creativity and resulting in less than zero connectivity to the employee's current performance or the business's needs.

> *Biz Tip* Creating Employee Development Plans is not a one-size-fits-all process.

It's clear that simply having an Employee Development Plan won't be enough. The successful implementation of such a program, or any employee retention process for that matter, will require planning, training, and careful execution.

Tips: What else do I need to know?

In your role as a manager (a.k.a. babysitter), you routinely manage and guide people, directly or indirectly, through the often choppy seas of daily professional life. This is a particularly important part of your role when it comes to the talented team members you don't want to lose. By developing a targeted approach for our employees and their professional development, we are working toward the following employee outcomes:

- Increased job satisfaction and retention
- Improved performance
- "Buy-in" on specific job goals and career objectives

Through these employee retention strategies, we are working toward the following company outcomes:

- A deeper talent pipeline or "bench"
- Improved succession planning
- Enhanced business sustainability and continuity
- A better bottom line

It's time to create employee retention programs that will achieve meaningful results in your organization. Here are a few methodologies for employee retention programs to move the ball forward toward these goals.

EMPLOYEE DEVELOPMENT PLAN

Designing an Employee Development Plan is an ongoing process and a crucial part of the employee life-cycle continuum. If the manager uses her experience effectively, she will listen more than talk, noting what each direct report says regarding workplace issues, as well as what is not said. The goal of designing these personalized plans is to set high standards for the employee by developing both soft skills (leadership, communication) and hard skills (job knowledge, industry expertise). The Employee Development Plans are unique and customized to each employee, and the company's goal is to improve performance throughout the organization, one employee at a time.

CONTINUING EDUCATION AND/OR PROFESSIONAL DEVELOPMENT

For both hard and soft skills, training and continuing education programs are widely used. These classes can be platform (live), virtual, or self-taught, depending on the nature of the skill and the format that is most effective for the content. The challenge typically for a business is the pure cost-benefit analysis that must occur—not only the cost of a class but also the time lost in the workplace. The "return on investment" in allowing an employee to learn something new or to become more proficient in a skill can sometimes be difficult to measure. However, the value to the employee is, in many ways, immeasurable.

SUCCESSION PLANNING

This retention tool is a process that involves recruiting key talent and developing that talent in preparation for increasingly elevated roles within the company. The goal is to identify and develop internal people who have potential to fill key business roles by cultivating their knowledge, skills, and abilities for more and more challenging roles. In this way, the company is preparing a talent pool of well-equipped employees who can fill vacancies of progressively higher caliber.

MENTORING

When effectively managed, mentoring programs offer an opportunity for junior staff to be aligned with members of senior management to grow business understanding and job knowledge at a faster pace. A mentoring relationship is intended to provide the mentee with a direct line of communication to upper management to seek guidance on both job-specific and company-specific questions. A mentor also gains from the mentoring relationship in terms of enhanced team building and personal satisfaction in working toward successful retention of the mentee.

MULTIDISCIPLINARY ROTATIONS

The benefits of positional rotation within an organization can be significant, both for the individual in expanding her skills and knowledge base and for the company in creating well-rounded employees who can handle cross-functional responsibilities. The challenge, however, is the very real problem this type of rotation creates for a business to take a productive employee off duty to learn on the job.

CAREER PATHS

The use of career paths as an employee retention tool is an effective method for providing clear pathways of progression for employees. Companies set career paths to establish a direction for upward mobility within an organization. One example is Schneider National Inc., a provider of premium truckload and intermodal services. One visit to Schneider's website—www.schneiderjobs.com/office-careers/career-paths—will make you a believer. Schneider has developed career paths for many of its key job progressions. This information is posted on the company website. Talk about motivating! For both applicants and employees, the clear message is that the company is interested in helping employees achieve their full potential, and the clearly identified career paths serve to inspire employees to continue moving up within the organization.

Tactics: Where do I go from here?

It's time to select your employee retention strategy and get started—or at least dust off your current program to update it. We're going to assist you in creating and implementing one of the employee retention tools, the Employee Development Plan. We are providing a framework below that you can customize, as needed, for each employee with whom you use it.

1. Hold the first meeting with the retention-worthy employee, and collaborate with the employee to determine a job/skill building pathway and to get the employee's buy-in.

2. Discuss key elements of the plan and identify key job functions and set goals accordingly; identify areas for soft skill enhancement and/or job-related learning; determine a game plan to achieve the selected goals; monitor progress; and meet regularly with the employee to check on progress and provide accountability.

3. For the follow-up meetings, start the discussion by reviewing the stated goals and action plan, evaluate progress, and determine a new action plan that continues to move the employee forward. Make sure that the employee understands this is a positive meeting with an eye toward personal development and successful job performance. When you follow up *when you said you would*, you validate the credibility of the program.

4. Assure the employee that your discussion regarding his individualized Employee Development Plan is confidential and will not be shared with his peers. The Employee Development Plan and related documentation is retained confidentially with other personnel records.

5. Be accountable. Closing the meeting on a positive note, with dates and times for follow-up, is a *must*! The reason for the meeting (really the reason for the employee development process as a whole) is to pinpoint areas for improvement, to develop a plan for addressing those identified gaps, and to make a commitment to work together for success.

BOTTOM LINE

To remain competitive in today's workplace, every organization needs to focus on retaining the best of the best. Whether your employees are considered high potential and heading for upper management or whether they are in need of a plan to move to the next level, an Employee Development Plan can be a powerful tool. Enable and empower your employees, engage them in the overall discussion, and envision a sustainable and focused workforce. Commit this truism to memory: "Employee engagement enhanced. Employee retention improved."

Create an environment in which employees recognize the effort being put into their own personal development within the job—and within the company. Within such an environment, employees are likely to work harder, achieve successful outcomes, and be more satisfied along the way. You'll be so glad you did.

CHAPTER 6

The Double-Edged Sword of Recognizing & Rewarding Employees

*There are two kinds of people: those who do the work
and those who take the credit. Try to be in the first group;
there is less competition there.*
—Indira Gandhi

There is an art to effectively recognizing employee performance, especially the work of those in departments whose efforts rarely get noticed. How do you make recognition meaningful, connect it to actual work activity, and involve employees in the process without making it a beauty pageant? Past experience tells us that the HR department is typically the keeper of the recognition program and is directed from above to ensure that employees are engaged and *want* such a recognition program. Contrary to management's lofty expectations, the general employee population may not really care about recognition programs, may even collectively roll their eyes when the "winner" is announced, but they will *always* complain about the lack of recognition if asked. That much has not changed. And so it goes.

There are very few ways to cleverly label our employee recognition programs other than those tied to time (Employee of the Month/Quarter/Year) or corner-office titles (Chairman's Award/President's Club) or departments (Top Sales/Customer Service) or company-related themes (Shining Star/Top Dog). No matter the name of the award or recognition, there should be some form of criteria to win. Therein lies the heart of the problem. Employee recognition is riddled with opportunities for the nonselected (recipient-challenged whiners) to cry foul. The goal of employee recognition is to reward a deserving employee and provide incentives to enhance performance. Such recognition can result in the opposite effect, though, nearly inciting a revolt.

By focusing on grandiose awards, we may unfortunately miss the reason behind employee recognition, which is to acknowledge and thank the employee for a job well done. This public thank-you doesn't have to be done from a stage; in fact, if an employee does something extraordinary, acknowledgment may be best received when it is delivered immediately and without ballyhoo. A handwritten note that acknowledges effort, an email blast that celebrates a job well done, or a personal pat on the back (not literally—touching is a topic for the harassment chapter) goes a long way in making an employee feel proud and appreciated. At some point in the history of corporate life, most companies' recognition programs became more about the giving of the award than about the effort and the commitment of the employee receiving the award.

MOJO *from* MASTERS

Suffice it to say, we strongly advocate one-on-one recognition to deserving employees. We all have a need for recognition and appreciation. This need can be satisfied by the smallest of tokens when delivered with sincerity in the right moment. A shout-out of appreciation at a staff meeting, written recognition in an email with a copy to the big boss, or a handwritten note with a gift card—these small but meaningful acknowledgments of a job well done carry a powerful impact.

This chapter is about recognition programs, however, so it is solely on that topic that we'll focus our remarks from here on out.

Tales: Am I the only sane person in the room?

I (Daren) had an experience early in my career with an employee recognition program at a company that employed several hundred employees. When I was chosen to be a representative on the Employee Recognition Committee, I believed that luck was on my side. How could I, as the new kid on the block, be soooooo fortunate to be selected for such a prestigious honor? Soon enough, though, it became clear that neither fortune nor luck had been on my side. This particular committee met monthly, collecting secret ballots as voted on by the office staff to determine the recipient of the Employee of the Month award. The winner was chosen based on very loose criteria, ending up as truly the person who was the most popular/well liked in the office. (NOTE: This was a numbers-driven business and actual work-product metrics could have been used to choose the winner. However, this had been tried in the past and no one on the committee ever liked the outcome. So, the committee had abandoned the numbers-only approach and replaced it with slightly vague and nebulous criteria.)

At the first monthly committee meeting attended by yours truly, a winner was chosen from the ballots, and as the new representative, it was my proud duty to take the information to the boss so that he could make the presentation. Imagine my surprise when the boss wasn't as thrilled as I was with the winner's name. The boss summarily vetoed the choice because, as he noted, while the winner had been reporting some decent numbers and while everyone liked the winner, the boss didn't.

Shaken, but not deterred, the committee regrouped and got the news (which they'd already expected, but why not send the new person to the lions and see what happens!). This forced a recount of the ballots and, magically, a new, more acceptable winner was chosen. You can already guess the impact this exercise had on not only those of us who were involved but also the employees who guessed the truth. The Employee of the Month program was a sham, without credibility, and lost momentum over time. Employees stopped voting, ceasing to care about an empty reward program, and we were left to dream up some other form of award system.

Let's take a look at a few other classic examples of employee recognition programs that have been implemented with varying levels of success.

POPULARITY CONTEST

Call it what you like, but we often end up basing recognition on the popularity of an employee. The company doesn't want a despised or less desirable participant to win an award, so we utilize more subjective criteria to determine a winner. In this way, the more widely liked (popular) employees receive recognition based on elusive or nonexistent criteria.

This methodology is more common than we'd like to admit, perhaps because it's an easier way to please the masses and discount those we don't like anyway. The program generally plugs along, but over time it is often abandoned because of employee apathy about its lack of providing recognition for meaningful achievements or because too many feelings get bruised along the way. The risk inherent in this methodology is that the truly rock-star performers (who maybe aren't equally popular) will be discouraged by never being recognized for solid achievement, and they'll take their heavy-hitting performance to greener pastures.

BATTING AVERAGE

This reward is all about the numbers, and the person with the best batting average wins. The advantage here is that the subjectivity has been removed and it's difficult to argue with the numbers. Numbers are numbers, right? Well . . . the challenge here is that the winner is recognized and rewarded no matter what it took to get to the top. If the winner got there on the coattails of others or with the assistance of others or used undesirable tactics to win, the result might be some disgruntled employees left behind in the dust. Once the dust settles, there will be those who are upset because they, likewise, did not receive their due recognition, or those who take issue with the tactics that led to the victory.

TOOT YOUR OWN HORN

Some recognition programs that are based on the criteria of the selection committee (or perhaps the committee itself) result in either the same people being recognized year after year or the failure to ever recognize the stellar wallflower. In such a system, the selection criteria allows for subjectivity; ultimately, the person who toots his own horn the loudest has the best chance of being recognized. We risk slighting our solid performers in favor of the showboaters.

TEAM RECOGNITION

Recognizing the entire team is a safe approach in that a group of people is recognized for its collective success. This sharing of the wealth encourages collaboration within a department or among departments, depending on the award criteria, and drives commitment to a common objective. As with all things, there are possible downsides, including the harder workers in the team becoming disenfranchised over their slacker teammates who received the same recognition for lesser effort. Remember working on group projects in the seventh grade? You did all the work. Yet, in the end, all the group members received A's. That's the feeling we're talking about.

Tips: What else do I need to know?

Here are a few questions to ask yourself as you consider what type of recognition program, if any, is right for your organization:

- Do we really need to recognize employees in a special way?

- Don't we already pay workers sufficiently for doing their job?

- Shouldn't we expect employees to exceed goals without the fluff?

It is true that we hope we've hired employees who have internal "on" switches that motivate them to work hard every day. It is also true, however, that almost everyone loves a little "attaboy" now and then. Recognition of effort is just one of the areas that may bring extra value to an employee. Among the myriad reasons why employees work for your company, there are many factors such as job satisfaction, growth opportunities, compensation, benefits, who they work with or for, the nature of the job, the location of the job, flexibility, and so on. We can't lose sight of that. So, we must strive for balance between the rewards that come from external recognition and those that are inherent in the job and workplace itself.

With that being said, let's address some of the nuances that lurk in the background as we discuss the things to consider when drafting and implementing an employee recognition program.

WIIFM (PRONOUNCED "WIFFEM")

Yes, the "What's In It for Me" aspect of any reward or recognition program is always there, silently preying on your good intentions. The current workplace environment includes many employees (Gen Yers, in particular) who have grown up receiving recognition for participation—yes, just simply showing up. Some of them attended schools where they had "no cut" sports and activities. This, again, meant everyone was deemed a winner. If they aren't rewarded under your recognition program, they may pack up their toys and go home.

On the other side of the spectrum, you may have seasoned participants (Baby Boomers or Gen Xers) who have a built-in component of skepticism or world-weary apathy toward the workplace and their colleagues. It can be tough to get buy-in from this group because the earlier answers to their WIIFM left them scarred and bruised. So the program has to have elements that can motivate or even appeal to most of the employee base. Know that you can't please everybody, but you can get a majority on board. Honest feedback from employees as to what type of rewards have the most meaning can help you build a program that addresses what matters most to them, not to those administering the program.

FAIRY DUST (A.K.A. NOT ANOTHER B.S. PROGRAM FROM MANAGEMENT)

In order for the program to work, employees must believe that it has credibility. This means that it is built on measurable criteria and that those involved have equal access to the brass ring. It can't be based on a moving target, nor can it have its results tracked in a subjective way. Many employees will be skeptical, and you will have to work that much harder to prove that the program is grounded in impartiality, with a justifiable outcome.

The program should be valid and sustainable, and the components should be based on solid reasoning that merges best practices gleaned from other companies, with input from the organization's own employees. In addition, the program should be fluid enough to adapt to changes in the company, the budget, the business units or individual roles themselves, and even the marketplace. There is really no reason to reinvent the wheel. Through a little research, you can find out what has worked well for your counterparts in other companies. Relay the fact that this is a new program founded on principles used successfully elsewhere, underscoring that you did your homework and have built the best possible mousetrap for the company.

AND THE WINNER IS . . .

The announcement of the winner(s) in the recognition program is another important element that reflects on the overall credibility of the program. *Oh, come on already*, you may be thinking. *How we present the award matters? Is there really a bad way to give recognition?* Yes, there is.

Follow this scene. Tom H. Employee has been selected as the Employee of the Year, which will be announced at the annual meeting. He is there in the auditorium in front of his peers and senior management. Tom is a grizzled (pissed-off, frankly) veteran of the corporate world, but he is obviously (and begrudgingly) pleased to receive his first ever notification that he is doing a good job. Tom's immediate boss, Sally Supervisor, is fairly new on the job and knows very little about Tom, but she sees this as her time on stage to display her winning personality. She turns to Tom and says, "Tom, you've been here at Company ABC a long time. Why you haven't won this award in the past is really beyond me. Your career started the day I left the eighth grade, and look at us now! I couldn't be more proud of your contribution to our unit." Mercifully, she at least read aloud the wording on the certificate before handing it to a stunned Tom. In this situation, the company had barely won Tom over to the program, for a slight moment, and then the moment was lost in translation due to a failure in the delivery of the message.

Biz Tip Don't let company representatives go onstage without a complete script, literally from "Hello" to "Good-bye," or the result can be disastrous.

Tactics: Where do I go from here?

You know what you have to do, don't you? If you don't have some form of recognition program in your organization, build one. If you do have one, review it for form, format, criteria, fairness, and general acceptance by the employee base. If the employees don't like it or, worse still, don't care, then it's time for a makeover. Ultimately, the challenge, as with everything we do, is in the execution of these programs.

Remember that the real reason we are rewarding employees for their behavior goes back to these four cascading principles about a successful and positive workplace:

1. Increased employee satisfaction means higher employee retention.

2. Higher employee retention means business stability and continuity.

3. Business stability and continuity means higher productivity.

4. Higher productivity means greater profits.

Admittedly, the math doesn't always carry through for each of these premises. For example, you may have higher employee retention of those people you simply can't get rid of, but that is a flaw elsewhere in your performance management process. For our purposes, the overall premise is solid. Having a more satisfied workforce decreases workplace friction, and that yields positive results.

So just what *does* a quality employee recognition-and-rewards program look like? Typically, a comprehensive program has the following key components.

DEFINED CRITERIA

The absolute worst thing we can do when creating a recognition program is to have one that is hollow. In other words, one where no foundation is discernible, which leads employees to question, "How the hell did you pick Mary for this award when my numbers are higher?" or "Interesting that John plays golf with the Boss so often . . . wait . . . is that why he won?" Be proactive and clearly define the award criteria, using as much in the way of measurable points as possible and thus defusing challenges to the system. Employees will buy into the program if they sense it is a valid and fair process. Clearly state what the company is doing and why the company is doing it, along with an explanation of the selection criteria and how employees are chosen for recognition.

Biz Tip   Make employee recognition and rewards a line item on your company's budget.

On the topic of budget, you will want to earmark money for two initiatives: to fund the recognition program and for "mad money" to allow for mini-celebratory rewards throughout the year. Now, let's go back to those one-off moments that don't require formal recognition at the annual dinner but should not go unnoticed. Celebrate the smaller successes with recognition that matches them: a handwritten thank-you note with movie tickets enclosed or a modest gift card for their favorite coffeehouse or an invitation to lunch. Make sure the rewards have meaning for the employees and reinforce the idea that this is the place to work because the company appreciates what they bring to the table.

VALUABLE AWARD

Awards are so plentiful nowadays that they seem to be given just for showing up! Don't think so? What about participation or service or attendance awards, to name a few? So let's assume you have been recognized for something. And now let's assume it was a big something you won at an annual meeting, like "Most Valuable Player" or "Employee of the Year." The expectation of a reward is set in your mind and in your heart. This is big, right?! It's got to be cash or a significant gift certificate or an all-expenses-paid trip or *something* of value. To have meaning, it's got to be more than a certificate or a plaque—although those are nice to have in addition to the reward. There is a delicate balance: Too little an award and it loses its meaning; too much, and it may not be sustainable. Ask employees for their input as to what they consider a valuable prize for various big awards. (We have talked extensively in this book about employee buy-in, and here is a prime place to use it.)

PRESENTATION

The nature and level of the recognition should dictate the setting for the presentation of the award/reward/recognition. For some employees, simply being acknowledged is enough; conversely, to others *zero* recognition is enough to send them packing. The determining factor as to how to present the recognition really relates to the underlying work required to achieve the award and the time frame. If the recognition is for a monthly award, the presentation and setting will be filled with significantly less pomp and circumstance. Annual recognition, on the other hand, usually accompanies a bigger event such as an annual dinner or separate function. We are not trying to overthink this process, but we *are* trying to avoid diluting the value of more significant achievements in relation to routine feats.

COMMUNICATION

When your organization's employee recognition-and-rewards program has been completed and approved and is ready for liftoff, pick the time to announce it carefully. Communicate the program's elements, criteria, timing, and awards through the use of all appropriate means. These will include, among others, the company intranet, posters in the break room, paycheck stuffers, hard copy document distribution, email blasts, or in-person meetings. This concerted effort will reinforce the importance of the program as well as the level of appreciation the company has for the employees. This is one of those "beyond the paycheck" moments—potentially a defining one—for the organizational culture, and everyone needs to embrace what you are trying to accomplish. Finally, if the recognition is akin to some type of workplace "lifetime achievement" award, consider outside media as an opportunity to not only announce the winner but also to promote the company's image to existing and future employees, customers, vendors, and other stakeholders.

BOTTOM LINE

If your company's employees are truly your greatest asset (as we say they are), then be creative in identifying ways to recognize and reward the desired performance, using employee input and defining a plan and executing a strategy within a predetermined budget. Employee recognition programs can be cost-effective ways to support positive workplace morale, enhance employee satisfaction and development, and drive better performance. By taking the time to carefully select appropriate criteria for the program, along with determining awards/rewards that align with the desired performance objectives, you can create a meaningful recognition process. Your employees will enjoy basking in the well-deserved limelight. All the while, don't miss an opportunity to say "thank you" and "you did a great job" along the way. You'll be so glad you did.

Part III

BABYSITTER: COACH AND COUNSEL

Let's shift our focus to other babysitting-type tasks in which the setting of rules is required, along with the need for guidance. In the workplace, these tasks are referred to as coaching and managing employees. Babysitters also find themselves needing to scold misbehavior or redirect a child's actions, much like attending to unwelcome or inappropriate behaviors in the workplace.

CHAPTER 7

The Best Work Coach Ever

"WHY CAN'T YOU JUST DO BETTER/BE LESS LOUSY TODAY?"

If your actions inspire others to dream more, learn more, do more, and become more, you are a leader.
—*John Quincy Adams*

Coaching covers a wide swath of activities. If you think about it, we all perform as coaches in various formats and for a variety of reasons at some point of almost every day of our professional lives. Whether as an HR professional, a manager of people (directly or indirectly), a work colleague or peer, or a business owner, we engage in coaching while at work. It may be a direct communication, such as giving additional instruction to an employee related to their performance on a recent project. Or it may be more subtle, such as a discussion with a peer in which we are talking the coworker off the career ledge before she jumps (or, alternatively, pushing her when she doesn't want to leap).

The term "coaching" and related terminology cover a wide variety of uses and meanings for each of us. To avoid confusion and to ensure that we are all on the same page, here's a brief glossary of *our* definitions of the vocabulary. (NOTE: We are laying groundwork here about relevant words that relate to a broad discussion about coaching. But the focus of this chapter will be on executive coaching and one-on-one coaching— terms of art we've defined below:

- **One-on-one Coaching:** Coaching between a designated management/HR representative and an employee to discuss targeted behaviors or job characteristics that either require correction or minor improvement, or to suggest recommendations for further development and enhancement of the employee's job performance. This one-on-one coaching effort is typically undertaken to help employees improve their performance, *not* for disciplinary reasons but to provide the employee with additional support.

- **Executive coaching**: Coaching focused on a select few individuals who hold high-level positions or aspire to such positions. The effort is typically undertaken by a skilled coach or well-trained manager to provide up-and-comers with additional tools, skills, and abilities to continue to grow in their current job with an eye toward future job opportunities/promotions within the company.

- **Counseling**: Typically a first step in a disciplinary matter, a verbal discussion (that is usually documented in writing) in which an employee receives specific guidance on an issue that most often relates to a performance deficiency, a policy violation, or some other workplace infraction.

- **Performance management**: A more formalized performance review program that typically integrates employees' job descriptions with their job performance, and is accompanied by the requisite performance appraisal documentation, regular communication, written action plans, and career guidance.

- **Progressive discipline**: The part of a company's tiered process that addresses unacceptable, inappropriate, or egregious behavior and the specific steps to remedy such behavior (sometimes using the levels of verbal warning, written warning, suspension, and termination).

- **Mentoring**: A formal program through which carefully selected (and trained) senior leaders provide one-on-one guidance to a junior or new member of the team through regular conversations to answer questions, as well as to cover specified training material relevant to the job, workplace, and industry.

Our goal is to provide a road map to assist you in the development of your own "coaching" skills as well as to discuss the different opportunities to use coaching (formal and informal) within your organization.

Before we go any further, let's do an exercise. When you consider the "best" or the "worst" coach (or boss) you have ever experienced—at work or in sports or some other venue—think about the attributes that are behind those labels. List those qualities in order of importance to you, remembering that "best" can't be because "he was the easiest on me" just like "worst" can't be "she was a no-good so-and-so." (Although your mental wandering may start out that way, don't end up there.) For our purposes, let's focus on "coaches" you have known in sports, extracurricular activities, and/or in the workplace.

Now, to get you started, think about those foundations of leadership you look for in another person and, ultimately, what you strive for in your own behavior as a leader. Elements such as honesty, integrity, fairness, a sense of humor, empathy, flexibility, and so on. We will come back to this exercise later, so make notes now.

The table below lists some of the most obvious "best coach" and "worst coach" attributes we've seen among bosses. (Note, even a good coach can be impatient or act arrogantly now and then. Nobody's perfect.)

Example	Good Attributes	Bad Attributes
Best work coach	• Genuinely believed in me • Communicated clear expectations • Provided specific feedback • Treated all team members with respect • Gave high praise when earned • Enthusiasm was contagious	• No patience • Arrogant

Example	Good Attributes	Bad Attributes
Worst work coach	• Spoke succinctly	• Never said a positive word • Focused on the negative • Two-faced—said one thing, did another • Bullied the weaker and newer people

Now write your own lists of the attributes exhibited by the best and worst coaches you've encountered in your workplace, in sports, and in extracurricular activities.

	Good Attributes	Bad Attributes
Best work coach		
Worst work coach		
Best sports coach		
Worst sports coach		
Best extracurricular coach		
Worst extracurricular coach		

Tales: Am I the only sane person in the room?

Let's start with an example of an employee who suffered from a severe case of woeisme ("woe is me") disease. As you might surmise, this employee blamed everyone else for her problems and had excuses for everything. Sound like anyone you know? This employee claimed that her supervisor was "harassing" her, and she raised a complaint with the HR Department. The basis for the harassment allegation related to the supervisor of Ms. Woeisme (hereafter referred to as Ms. W) asking her to report to work on time, meet department production standards, and avoid personal calls during work.

With regard to being on time, Ms. W explained that she's really not a morning person, she often gets stuck in traffic, and her job can really be done any time of the day. In response to being told she needs to arrive to work on time, Ms. W replied, "I really don't see the big deal about reporting to work late so long as I show up and get my job done. I mean, let's face it, my supervisor's just really uptight."

With regard to the production standards in her department (the same numbers that everyone in the department was expected to meet), Ms. W claimed this was apparently how her supervisor planned to "crush" her. She agreed her performance was not hitting the mark, and that others seemed to hit the numbers, but it just all seemed so unfair.

With regard to the numerous personal calls made during work time, she simply said she had personal matters to attend to and such rules were "stupid in the first place."

Biz Tip How can you straighten out a difficult situation? Through performance management? Progressive discipline? Coaching? Maybe all of these.

Since the performance issues were brought to light as a result of the harassment complaint raised by Ms. W, this matter must be carefully addressed. Interestingly (and unfortunately), the basis for Ms. W's harassment allegations actually highlighted performance deficiencies that her supervisor had apparently been trying to manage. However, we shouldn't throw this over the fence and address it through performance management or progressive discipline quite yet. We must be careful to avoid retaliation claims under such circumstances. First, a thorough investigation into Ms. W's harassment complaint must be undertaken and completed. For the sake of this example, let's say an investigation occurs and it was determined that there was no harassment. Now, it's time for the parties involved (Ms. W, her direct supervisor, and perhaps others in her department who may have been brought in during the investigation) to play nice. This isn't always easy. The manager is likely angry (or worse) at Ms. W for making such claims that portrayed her performance problems as poor performance by the manager. Coworkers may also be mad that Ms. W hasn't been doing her job and yet appears to be getting a free pass.

Following the conclusion of the investigation, one approach would be to offer Ms. W some one-on-one work coaching. Who should be the coach? At this juncture, it might be best to provide the coaching through someone other than her direct supervisor. Perhaps someone from HR, or a manager higher up the chain of command in her department, or even a coach hired from outside the organization would do.

The purpose of this coaching will be to address the performance matters that came to light during the investigation and to work toward getting the employee on track to meet legitimate job expectations. The coaching will likely include:

- A discussion of the performance expectations that are not being met

- An explanation as to the legitimacy of those expectations and how those job requirements fit into department and company goals

- A discussion of the job expectations in relation to the consistency of enforcement throughout the department

- The development of a realistic plan for achieving improved performance

- A time frame during which to monitor and evaluate the achievement of the established work goals/improved performance

In this example, the one-on-one coaching would be used to address specific work issues—with one employee—with the goal to achieve improved performance and have a more engaged employee. With any luck, this will also result in improved relations between the supervisor and employee as well as within the department as a whole. If the coaching doesn't result in the desired outcome, the matter will likely become one to be handled—either through the performance management process or progressive discipline. (NOTE: These processes may also run on parallel tracks—or run right smack into each other—depending on the circumstance.) For example, you may ultimately have this employee receive one-on-one coaching for the purpose of improving her job performance, while she also might need to be placed on progressive discipline if her chronic tardiness does not improve.

Let's compare the use of one-on-one coaching from the previous example to a very distinctive circumstance where coaching—executive coaching—will be a key component of the employee's career development. This example involves a large corporation in the Midwest, with more than five thousand employees, where the executive management team believed strongly in the idea of promoting employees from within whenever possible. This philosophy fostered an environment where employees became invested in their jobs, because they could see that standout performance really led to future opportunity—promotions, increased responsibilities, higher compensation, and career progression.

As part of this philosophy, executive coaching became an important tool. Employees who were on track for significant upward movement in the organization were often offered executive coaching as part of their training and development. Other employees, who were working in jobs that stretched their capabilities, were also given executive coaching to arm them with skills necessary for the immediate tasks at hand. In this environment, "coaching" didn't mean you were in trouble; it meant you were on your way to the top. This coaching was delivered by either a well-trained HR professional from within the organization or an outside executive coach.

Need any further convincing that coaching can have a

positive impact? By establishing a sustainable coaching methodology in tandem with your overall performance management program, your organization should see real dividends paying off. Train the leadership in methodologies that enhance the employee experience, reinforce that training, and make sure the employee base understands that the company is reinvesting in the workplace. Get to know individual employees through coaching and you'll also learn a lot about the work environment as a whole.

Tips: What else do I need to know?

Grab the worksheet you completed at the start of the chapter about good and not-so-good coaches you've encountered. Wait . . . did you really write stuff down? If not, do it now.

Make two columns with the data you collected: Title the first column "Good Coach Characteristics" and the other "Bad Coach Characteristics." You will note that both the good and the bad coaches usually have both good and bad characteristics. Once you have your lists compiled, put your pencil down.

Here are ours:

Good Coach Characteristics	Bad Coach Characteristics
Genuinely believed in me	No patience
Communicated clear expectations	Arrogant
Provided specific feedback	Never said a positive word
Treated all team members with respect	Focused on the negative
Gave high praise when earned	Two-faced—said one thing, did another
Enthusiasm was contagious	Bullied the weaker and newer people
Spoke succinctly	

Your two lists can now serve as your inspiration: The good list will be a regular reminder of the characteristics that you are striving to develop as you hone your coaching skills; the bad list can help you avoid those characteristics that you found unappealing or that made it easy for you to disregard anything that particular coach said. Keep these taped to the inside of your planner (old school!) or stored in your mobile device for easy access as a reminder about what you are striving for in your work interactions as a coach to others. Remember to refer to your list often.

As you reflect on characteristics of people who have coached you, let's take a closer look at different coaching styles. Some of these we hope to never encounter on our professional pathway, and others we'd like to emulate.

COACH SISTER MARY SUNSHINE

Being positive is a good thing. However, it is possible to have a coach who is *too* positive. Oddly enough, being too nice or too positive can have its downsides, which doesn't help you either. Years ago, I (Daren) had such a manager. She was one of the nicest people you could ever hope to meet and someone you would really want to work for, do your best for, and deliver the goods for. That is exactly what happened. I liked working for her, I did my best for her, and I delivered the goods (or so I thought). Then, through my own digging I realized I was doing some things wrong, but I wasn't being corrected, nor was I learning, growing, or ascending the corporate ladder. I was gaining "participation points" just for being at work and trying really hard and being a good teammate. I loved my job and Sister Mary Sunshine, but everyone in our department had actually fallen behind. There was no stick; it was all carrot. It's a pleasant enough environment, but over time the lack of challenge or being required to stretch oneself can become monotonous and stale.

THE EVIL ONE

Imagine a coach exactly the opposite of Sister Mary Sunshine and you have the Evil One. Unfortunately, each of us has probably experienced this coach. This type differs from our first example because he uses only one methodology to get results—steady negative. When the Evil One decides you are not worthy, you should go ahead and leave. The Evil One likes to operate in public when dressing down an employee. The Evil One takes being a hard-nosed coach to a new level— the style is driven by promising negative consequences for underperformance. The threats are severe and employees can become paralyzed under the negative pressure.

Picture a coaching session in which the Evil One requires a report on the past week's activities related to something that isn't even a stated goal. The employee can barely breathe, much less put together two sentences in response. Finally, the employee mutters an attempted response that sounds like a bluff. The Evil One senses fear and bluffing, so he pounces. He spews phrases like "You are personally costing the company time and money" and "Am I supposed to do *your* job too?" and my favorite "Obviously your lack of ability got you this far, but no more." Is this coaching for successful outcomes? I think not. Is it a missed opportunity to have a positive impact on the employee's career? You bet.

Let's move to where we want to be, namely, neither Sister Mary Sunshine nor the Evil One. Pull out the list of positive characteristics of your best coaches ever. That's where you want to start.

Tactics: Where do I go from here?

Here are the questions you will need to answer to determine how to best utilize the various types of coaching in your workplace:

- What goals are we trying to achieve through coaching?
  - For a problem employee, your goal is to get the employee back on track through identifying the issues and developing solutions.
  - For an employee with performance shortcomings, your goal is to assess the deficiencies and provide steps for improvement.
  - For a stellar employee, your goal is to build upon existing skills and give him or her new proficiencies for upward mobility in the organization.
  - For employees as a whole, your goal is to help them improve, grow, and achieve.
- Who should provide the coaching?
  - An outside coach/consultant
  - Internal resources: HR representative, supervisor, or higher-level manager

- How will we approach the delivery of the coaching?
  - On an as-needed basis, when we identify a situation where coaching could be useful
  - Through a formal program, when we decide to make coaching one of our institutional go-tos

Employee coaching can be a value-added commodity that, when used effectively, will result in higher employee satisfaction and retention, increased productivity, and an improved bottom line for the business. If we're lucky, various managers in our company inherently have the coaching gene. But, as the saying goes, "If it were easy, everybody would do it." What if we don't have coaches or if they simply haven't been adequately trained? Then, we will hire outside talent or work harder to build from within.

Let's assume we've taken on the task of building from within. Our goal will be to help designated managerial personnel find their "inner coach." Once trained, the coaches can engage in one-on-one coaching as needed. (Keep in mind they may ultimately become sufficiently proficient as a coach to also deliver a formal coaching program.) If you don't subscribe to the DIY (do-it-yourself) craze, there are many continuing education and professional-development courses that are instructed by people with impressive credentials. You can send your people out for training or bring the courses in-house.

Yes? You are up for the challenge? Stay with us. Otherwise, take five and jump to the next section in this chapter.

The key elements for anyone who wants to engage in meaningful, one-on-one, informal coaching include:

- **Customized solutions**: The coach-to-be needs to be prepared to know that their advice giving, solution creating, and performance building will sometimes require thoughtful planning and other times will be on the fly. Some coaching conversations can happen very spontaneously, and others will occur only after careful consideration and development of an action plan.

- **Effective listening**: This means more ears and less mouth. Coaches must develop a strong aptitude for deftly listening to their "coachee." It is here that good coaches distinguish themselves. By giving the employee the opportunity to describe her thinking on a particular matter, the coach can gain understanding, insight, and clarity before developing solutions or answers. An interactive conversation also allows the coach to listen for what is said as well as what is not said. In this role, the coach does less lecturing from on high; she and the employee converse in order to come to a better mutual understanding.

- **Constructive positivity**: Yep, we made this up. Sure, you can use it. Constructive positivity refers to constructive criticism or instruction by a coach to push improvement, delivered with a dose of positive encouragement. The goal of the coaching opportunity is to create a positive, forward-moving experience for the employee. Granted, there may be difficult topics to cover and, sometimes, conflict may arise. In that case, the coach should target the message, be precise, and avoid being preachy. Coaching conversations focus on behaviors and performance, not direct attacks on the employee.

Let's pause for just a moment and look at what one of these coaching conversations might look like.

> **Coach**: Employee Y, I am looking forward to working with you on developing some communication styles that may enhance your interactions within your department.

> **Employee**: This is really a bunch of nonsense. I'm still not even sure why I'm here. Am I in trouble?

> **Coach**: You are not in trouble per se. But your manager has identified what he believes are communication breakdowns by you in your interactions with others in your department.

> **Employee** (*getting heated*): Well, that's just B.S.! My manager is the one with the problem!

> **Coach**: Let's stop there for a minute. You are starting to raise your voice with me. Do you realize what you sound like to others when you raise your voice?

> **Employee**: Uh, no, sorry. I think I just get irritated when someone tells me I'm not doing something the right way.

> **Coach**: Okay. I understand that reaction. But before you go on the offensive, it would be wise to hear the other person out first.

> **Employee**: Uh-huh. Okay. I'm listening.

> **Coach**: What else irritates you?

> **Employee**: I don't like it when my boss or others correct me. I've been doing this job a long time.

Coach: What does your boss correct you about?

Employee: It will usually be something about a change in the production quality.

Coach: Does that have an impact on the way you do your job?

Employee: Yeah, it means I'll need to change the machine calibration and have to stop mid-run.

Coach: Is your boss really correcting you?

Employee: No, it's more about the run. I just don't want to be bothered and have to stop mid-run.

Coach: So, I hear you saying that you're really bothered by stopping the run, not by being corrected by your boss. Do I have that right?

Employee: Yeah, I guess.

Coach: Then let's focus on two things: (1) what gets you irritated, and (2) what steps can you take to manage that. We need to identify the triggers, work through other ways to respond, and then practice your new ways to respond. The goal will be to arm you with different behavioral responses, which could lead to better communication and interaction with your boss and in your department. Are you on board?

Employee: Sure. I'll give it a try.

Coach: We'll keep meeting after this to see how it's going. We can always modify our strategy if it isn't getting the results we're after.

Employee: Okeydokey.

FOLLOW-UP

Coaching is an ongoing process. It ultimately comes to a conclusion because the issue is resolved, the performance problem is cured, or the training/lessons have been conveyed. Part of a coach's job is to measure improvement or progress toward a goal, while having a willingness to tweak the approach if needed. What happens if the coaching results in the desired outcome? You celebrate success! When it works—and it will—let the employee and others involved know. We are all in this together, and the more success stories we can acknowledge and honor, the better the organization will be.

BOTTOM LINE

In addition to your regular day job and associated tasks, your role as a coach will be intermittently intertwined with duties that may require wearing any or all of the following hats: adviser, teacher, motivator, critic, instructor, monitor, counselor, and recognition distributor. You will wear them well. Keep in mind that coaching can improve the performance and retention of all employees, ranging from struggling and average performers to your next shining star. Coaching for successful outcomes is the journey we are on, and it never stops. We are bolstering employee morale, increasing job performance, and enhancing our employee retention—all by engaging ourselves (and others) in coaching. Take the time to do it right, one employee at a time. You'll be so glad you did.

CHAPTER 8

Employees Gone Wild

HARASSMENT, DIRTY JOKES
& OTHER BOORISH BEHAVIOR

A word to the wise ain't necessary—
it's the stupid ones that need the advice.
—Bill Cosby

What happened to fun in the workplace? Remember the good ol' days when dirty jokes, racy comments, and derogatory slurs were taken with a grain of salt? Everyone seems so darn uppity now. No one can take a joke anymore. Or . . . were those *really* the good ol' days?

What's the big deal if someone tells a group of work friends a dirty joke while chatting in the break room? Who really cares if someone sends a racy picture from a work email to a close friend? Really, they were just kidding around in the first place. Everyone needs to lighten up. Right? Well, it's not that easy.

Fun still exists in the workplace. But the ground rules have definitely changed. The old view as to what was acceptable in terms of words and behaviors no longer holds true. To be philosophical about it, we are no longer in the position to cast the stone in the pond and ignore selected ripples. We have to pay attention to all of the ripples.

Before we go any further, let's talk about terminology and be sure we're on the same page.

- **Discrimination**: Adverse treatment against an employee or applicant regarding a term or condition of employment on the basis of the person's protected status (i.e., race, religion, age, sex, color, national origin, pregnancy, disability, genetic information, military status, or citizenship). Protected status is defined by both federal and state law, and the categories vary from state to state.

- **Harassment**: Unwelcome conduct on the basis of protected status including race, religion, color, age (40 and over by federal law), sex, national origin, disability or genetic information in which the conduct rises to the level of altering the conditions of employment or creating a hostile workplace environment.

  - Sexual Harassment: One form of harassment that includes unwelcome sexual advances, requests for sexual favors, and other verbal, visual, or physical conduct of a sexual nature. Such conduct may constitute sexual harassment when: (1) submission to such conduct is made either explicitly or implicitly a term or condition of an individual's employment;

(2) submission to or rejection of such conduct by an individual is used as the basis for employment decisions affecting such individual; or (3) such conduct has the purpose or effect of unreasonably interfering with an individual's work performance by creating an intimidating, hostile, or offensive working environment.

- **Retaliation**: Retaliation occurs when employers take adverse employment actions against employees because they engage in protected activities, such as asserting a complaint or providing assistance in an investigation.

We are focusing on the "H word"—harassment—in this chapter. It's also important to understand that there are two different types of unlawful workplace harassment: quid pro quo and hostile work environment.

QUID PRO QUO

"Quid pro quo" literally means *this for that*—for instance, when someone with managerial/supervisory authority requires sexual favors/behavior from a subordinate (direct or indirect) in exchange for some term or condition of employment. This could include a promise for a reward in the workplace, such as a new job, a promotion or a raise in exchange for sexual favors. Conversely, this type of harassment could include a threat, such as termination, pay decrease, or demotion, if the sexual favor requests or advances are rejected. Even if the promise or threat is not realized, this behavior may still constitute sexual harassment.

HOSTILE WORK ENVIRONMENT

A hostile work environment is the most common type of harassment. Hostile work environment involves unwelcome behavior, comments, or actions of a sexual nature (or based on certain other protected status) that unreasonably interferes with work performance or creates a hostile or offensive workplace environment. A hostile work environment does not literally mean "hostile" in the sense of hostility or anger; it means that the offensive behavior, based on protected status as defined by law, has risen to a level that impedes an employee's ability to perform his or her job.

Keep these two key points in mind:

- Behaviors that can result in the creation of a sexually harassing hostile work environment include dirty jokes, comments of a sexual nature, and sexually suggestive comments, pictures, cartoons, and videos, along with sexual banter or other conversation of a sexual nature.

- Behaviors that can result in the creation of a hostile work environment can include jokes, comments, derogatory pictures or statements made on the basis of protected status, beyond sex, to include religion, race, age, national origin, disability, etc.—all of which fall under the rubric of protected status. This is another good opportunity to check with your employment lawyer for the specific list of protected categories applicable within the jurisdiction where your workplace is located.

As many of you know from experience, the role of business owner, manager, supervisor, or HR professional has changed over time, from being a bystander (or possibly engaging in the impropriety) to the role of law enforcement (a.k.a. riot police). Typically, we are the ones who have the least amount of fun at company events (even though we planned them), especially where alcohol is served, because we are always on duty, and our friends in other corporate departments know it. Somewhere in between police and patsy is the place where we hope to create and sustain a positive, non-harassing workplace environment in a way that is both palatable and appreciated—*without* a hush falling over the break room every time we enter.

MOJO *from* MASTERS

Year after year I (Julie) had the good fortune of delivering the keynote speech at our law firm's annual partner meeting. Well, "keynote" might be a stretch. Alright, alright. I conducted our non-harassment training. Over time, the running joke at the meetings became who would draw the short straw to sit with me the rest of the weekend. It's lonely at the top.

Tales: Am I the only sane person in the room?

As the unofficial keeper of the company's moral compass and very official company tattletale, an HR professional, a member of management, or anyone with supervisory responsibilities is tasked with enforcing the company's policies against behaviors that might constitute harassment. As we've said, this fact often makes HR staff and company supervisors a fairly unpopular lot.

Consider the following scenarios to see just how far we've come (or not) in creating harassment-free work environments.

PIG IN LIPSTICK

No amount of lipstick could have prettied up and saved this particular employee. In this situation, the employee was caught sending dirty jokes (sexual in nature) and inappropriate pictures (more of the same) from her work email. She knew of the company's non-harassment policy, and she also understood that jokes or pictures that contained sexual content were not in keeping with that policy. However, she was under the mistaken impression that she would be okay sending such material to a close friend *outside* the company. Wrong.

Two other things she got wrong: (1) It is never a good idea to keep inappropriate material on a company-provided system, and (2) it is never a good idea to send inappropriate material through company email. Remind your employees not to fall victim to the false premise that such behavior is *okay* when the material is sent to a close friend or someone whom they assume will not be offended.

This particular employee's bad behavior was exposed by her own carelessness. Instead of sending her off-color email to her intended recipient, a close friend, she sent it to a coworker— purely by accident. No ill will here. She inadvertently clicked the wrong name in her email drop-down box. Big difference. Big mistake.

The company later received notice of a lawsuit from the unintended recipient. During the discovery process, it was uncovered that this employee actually had megabytes of inappropriate material stored on her company computer, and her routine email traffic and Internet browsing (all during work hours) raised many eyebrows.

Biz Tip   Where there is smoke, there is often fire. Over the years, we have found that when someone admits to doing something once, it's likely there's a lot more to be discovered. But your independent investigation into allegations must be undertaken with objectivity and without pre-determined notions about the outcome.

HAIL TO THE "CHIEF"

In this story we are visited once again by Bad Boss ("Chief"), who is actually a very charismatic and likable leader in his organization. The company is starting Day 2 of its company-wide non-harassment training. Looking as though she's just seen a ghost, the HR director greets the trainer in the parking lot. "I think I need to conduct a harassment investigation," she says. "What happened?" asks the trainer (already sensing it's a question better left unanswered). The HR director hands the trainer a manila folder that contains stacks of printed emails. "After the training yesterday, this was given to me by one of the administrative assistants in Customer Service." A quick glance at the emails revealed that Chief's name routinely appeared as the sender. It quickly became apparent why the color had drained from the HR director's face. The emails read like a Harlequin romance novel.

Biz Tip Sometimes, non-harassment/discrimination training may lead to an immediate increase in internal complaints of harassing/discriminatory behavior. HR and the management team need to be aware that this is a possibility. The upshot is that a positive outcome will result if inappropriate behaviors that may have continued undetected are actually brought to light. In this way, the company can address the issues and prevent them from otherwise continuing.

The previous scenario illustrates behavior that bestows upon its recipient one of the most difficult challenges out there—namely, when a member of management (or, even worse, the top dog) engages in unwelcome or inappropriate sexual comments or conduct toward a subordinate. The lucky recipient of the complaint will need to be sure that the matter is addressed, which requires an investigation into the alleged wrongdoing, a determination about what occurred and whether the conduct violated company policy, and a decision about what, if any, disciplinary response is required. Additional questions that may arise include: What is the best way to prevent a recurrence? What, if any, intermediary action is necessary for the alleged victim throughout the process? Have there been prior similar occurrences, and how were those matters handled?

These situations are challenging enough. But when the allegations involve a manager/supervisor/executive-level employee, the stakes get even higher. It's difficult to determine the best and most effective approach to managing the situation when the ultimate decision maker in the organization is under scrutiny. Our best advice to you is to reach out for assistance. You can consider contacting any one or more of the following: the company board of directors; outside legal counsel; higher-up member of HR; member of the executive/management team; or someone as high up the chain as possible. You'll want to select someone who will not interfere with the process or jeopardize the legitimacy of the outcome. Still glad you took this job? We are.

Tips: What else do I need to know?

Labeling defamatory or prejudicial conversation as satire doesn't make it acceptable in the workplace. The "fun" is sucked out of "funny" in the workplace when the joke, comment, picture, action, etc., is offensive or belittling to another person and that behavior is based on one of the categories protected by law. True enough, a joke about an employee's protruding nose hairs or another employee's annoying habit of biting nails during a meeting or another's propensity to break into his college fight song prior to game weekends may be irritating (or even described as "harassing" in a general sense). However, such behavior does not in and of itself constitute harassment that is prohibited by law.

Wait a minute! That can't be right. How many times have you heard someone complain that they're being "harassed" by a work colleague, citing silly, nonsensical, irritating behaviors or comments as the reason for their complaint? You know who you are (actually, these "offenders" usually don't). The cubicle neighbor who pops her head into your cubby every ten minutes for a "neighbor check"—annoying? Yes. Irritating? You bet. Unlawful harassment? Nope.

No matter how much the employee's conduct annoys another person in the workplace, the behavior will be deemed actionable harassment *only* if it is *offensive on the basis of a category protected by law*. So, employees are allowed to annoy away . . . they just can't cross the line into comments, jokes, pictures, or behaviors that could be offensive on the basis of protected status as defined by law.

Biz Tip   Protected status for harassment under federal law includes race, color, religion, age (40 and over), sex, national origin, disability, and genetic information. Don't forget that state and local laws vary and may have additional protected categories such as sexual orientation, familial status, and so forth. Be sure to check your own state and local laws.

When it comes to comments or behaviors that are offensive or derogatory on the basis of protected status, the line between what was once acceptable and what's currently acceptable has been drawn with greater clarity. Despite our increased understanding and heightened awareness about the permissibility (or prohibition) of certain conduct in the workplace, people seem to find the line in the sand, erase it, and move forward—again and again and again and then again—until they're stopped by a force beyond themselves, such as a colleague, HR, or the boss.

Another key element in a hostile work environment harassment claim is that the perpetrator of such bad behavior may not realize—or doesn't understand or has forgotten—that the behavior/comment is evaluated through the eyes and ears of the recipient. Ill intent is not a requirement to prove harassment; in fact, bad motives on the part of the perpetrator rarely exist. The perpetrator may be well intended. However, it's the recipient of the "inappropriate" stuff who largely holds the keys to the kingdom. For example, think through the intent behind the behavior of each party below. The intent doesn't matter; the content and context of the behavior do.

"YOU HAD ME AT 'HELLO.'"

There is a blossoming (although under-wraps) office romance between Bad Boss and Employee. The relationship hits the skids. After the romance goes south, Employee becomes so (fill in the blank) hurt, upset, angry, jealous, mad, vindictive, scorned, obsessed, bewildered, desperate, lost, emotional, agitated—you get the idea—from the demise of the relationship that she then goes on the attack. Selective recall sets in. Memories become distorted. What once was, no longer is. What used to be a "relationship" is now portrayed as behavior involving unwelcome sexual comments, unwanted sexual behavior, etc. Bad Boss, once the paramour, is now cast as the perpetrator of all things unwanted and unwelcome. Think quid pro quo harassment. Not the behavior Bad Boss intended, nor the characterization of the relationship he would have predicted (but should have).

THE GIFT THAT KEEPS ON GIVING

Picture this: Funny jokes and inappropriate pictures are being circulated through email within a department. The written communication is reinforced by the racy jokes and derogatory banter routinely imparted among department members while getting their first cup of morning coffee (company-provided Starbucks, mind you: half-caff, extra hot, room for cream, French roast). At some point, one of the coffee-adoring, joke-loving, so-called friends in the department grows (fill in the blank) weary, tired, offended, insulted, upset, affronted, snubbed, disparaged, slighted, or otherwise left out, and he decides to report the behavior, which has undoubtedly crossed the line on many occasions. And the primary perpetrator against whom the complaint is raised can only think to herself, *"I didn't mean to offend anyone. I was only kidding, can't anyone take a little joke? I wasn't saying it to be offensive, I was being funny."* Bear in mind, none of these sentiments presents a victorious defense.

And so it goes. These examples provide an understanding of the circumstances under which people may create a harassing environment without necessarily *intending* to.

Tactics: Where do I go from here?

As evolved as we'd like to think people are, we know that there are, and will likely always be, behavioral challenges in the workplace, whether we have employees who simply don't know any better, don't care, have a momentary lapse in judgment, or simply underestimate the impact of what they've said or done. To stay ahead of the curve, we must carry the flag, walk the talk, and chew gum all at the same time. On second thought, you can forget the gum-chewing part. We must commit to having a harassment-free work environment by cultivating a workplace where everyone understands the type of behavior that is prohibited and knows that the directive will be enforced. Let's address the necessary elements to promote a harassment-free work atmosphere.

Biz Tip   Key elements to create a harassment-free workplace environment

- Written non-harassment policy
- Harassment complaint procedure
- Non-harassment training

WRITTEN NON-HARASSMENT POLICY

The company should have a definitive statement regarding non-harassment in the workplace. Period. The organization's definitive statement on harassment should be fully communicated and the message reinforced on a regular basis. If the organization doesn't have such a statement, *get one!* Enforcing a non-harassment policy is a reasonable, proactive approach to ensuring that effective and consistent communication is occurring across the organization, that the employees know the company is committed to a workplace free from harassment, and that consequences exist should anyone violate the policy.

> **Biz Tip** Remember, it's not enough for a company to simply post its non-harassment/non-discrimination policy on the wall; the message should become part of the company's cultural DNA.

The policy needs to contain the following elements:

- Provide definitions of harassment, discrimination, and retaliation. Make it clear such conduct is prohibited.

- Provide the definition of quid pro quo harassment and hostile work environment.

- Give an explanation of what constitutes prohibited behavior and provide examples of the prohibited conduct.

- Provide a list of all of the protected categories under federal and applicable state law to make it clear what the bases are for prohibited conduct.

The policy also needs to address harassment complaint procedures:

- State a requirement that supervisors and employees report incidents, even if the behavior isn't directed toward them, and regardless of whether the reporter thinks the company is already aware or that someone else may have reported it.

- Establish a reporting mechanism for complaints to be raised, along with both formal and informal means for reporting.

- Provide options for reporting so employees and supervisors have more than one available avenue for reporting a complaint/incident (permit a range of channels, including anonymous).

- Give details about the company's expectation that other types of intimidation, hostility, or other offensive behavior based on protected status that may interfere with an employee's work performance will also not be tolerated.

- Explain that an investigation will be undertaken to determine the underlying circumstances and that appropriate corrective or preventive measures will be taken, if deemed necessary.

- Provide an anti-retaliation statement to affirm that no retaliation will result from exercising rights under the policy.

- State an explanation of the disciplinary consequences that may result for policy violations.

Biz Tip Use the preceding bullet points as a checklist to review the sufficiency of your company's written non-harassment policy.

NON-HARASSMENT TRAINING

The policy and the complaint procedure are of no value if you fail to publish, communicate, execute, and reinforce them. After creating the policy and the procedure, execute an integrated plan to disseminate the information, including inclusion of the non-harassment policy and the complaint procedure in other written documents, such as the employee handbook. Look for other ways to reinforce your harassment-free work environment, be it on signs throughout the building, via HR email blasts, or through more frequent training.

Speaking of training, make sure your company is conducting training sessions routinely for everyone in the organization, from top to bottom, to establish the company's commitment to being proactive in ensuring that employees are well informed on the company's non-harassment/non-discrimination policy and complaint procedure. Pursuant to recent federal court decisions, it has become imperative that companies do more than just hand out a policy and have a signed acknowledgment for the policy. It is wise to conduct non-harassment training (including a discussion of non-discrimination and anti-retaliation) for all new hires and routinely (we suggest annually) for current employees. The training can be delivered through company-wide or department-wide in-person sessions or through online, self-directed training programs.

In addition, you should also provide additional training for management-level employees (HR, managers, supervisors, etc.) to whom complaints may be made to ensure that they understand their responsibilities and how to handle the report.

These persons will likely need to be given direction on how to respond to the complainant and where to take the report internally for handling. The actual follow-up, such as an investigation and determination of any disciplinary outcome, is usually handled in a centralized way, either through the HR department or other delegated management representative(s). Your managerial people need to understand exactly how the process works in your organization. All of the effort that you put into this process will pay dividends not only for defensive purposes but also to enhance your corporate culture going forward.

BOTTOM LINE

Why, in this day and age, are we still talking about harassment in the workplace, especially when it seems to be such an obvious topic to the average person on the street? Because inappropriate behavior still exists and is now even more potentially dangerous than ever to a company's reputation. In particular, due to the speed with which information goes viral through social media and other forms of cybercommunication, companies are more vulnerable than ever to public image meltdowns at the hands of a scoundrel employee who perpetrates bad behavior.

The influencers and the keepers of a company's ethical and moral behavior (we are talking to you), must understand that employees are reluctant to change their behavior, especially if they don't feel they are doing anything wrong. It is incumbent upon us to keep moving the message forward and instill the belief in our workplaces that professional respect is a key factor in achieving success. Actions must match the words that are spoken. People will see the consistency between word and deed. It will require you to commit to play by the rules and, at times, be slightly unpopular. In the long run, you'll be so glad you did.

CHAPTER 9

The "Joys of Management"

DELEGATING RESPONSIBILITIES, ACCEPTING
UNDUE BLAME & ASSIGNING MISPLACED CREDIT

*By working faithfully eight hours a day, you may eventually
get to be the boss and work twelve hours a day.*
—*Robert Frost*

You may or may not believe this, but there is no pure bliss in the management of other people. There, we've said it. Okay, some aspects are rewarding, like connecting opportunity with the employee and watching the latter succeed. The task of managing people can have its moments of absolute elation: seeing an employee you hired and mentored ascend up the ranks or witnessing a long-term employee receive accolades for achieving certain successes that you've helped guide and shape.

But there's another side to management, isn't there? Those moments when someone is looking for the scapegoat and you, as the manager, become it. Or those times when a project goes marvelously under your leadership and you don't receive even so much as a "nice job." But, hey, that's why you get paid the big bucks.

Have you ever made this statement: "If I get to be the boss, I will . . . /will not ever . . ."? Of course you have. When we first start our careers or any new job, we are full of hope. The world is open and possibilities are endless. Then the second day of employment arrives and you wonder where all the nice people went. You say to yourself, *They said I would love it here forever!* Whenever the candidate courtship ends, you may be exposed to new realities that hadn't been previously disclosed. You've been made a manager of the biggest group of underdogs because you seemed up to the challenge. Or you have become the direct report to a manager who views herself as your new lord and master.

So let's focus on how to overcome unforeseen obstacles and design a way to create an environment in which managers (including you) can achieve optimum performance.

Tales: Am I the only sane person in the room?

There are many types of managers—you know, Good Boss and Bad Boss types. And we can learn something from every one of them: ways to do things or not do them, styles that are effective or not effective, communication that works or doesn't work. Remember that as managers we are influenced by external forces—the organization itself, the culture, our peers and underlings, the company's structure, the company's stated goals, even our own supervisor—as well as by internal forces—our own prior experiences, previous successes and failures, core beliefs and ethos, and personal biases or personality traits.

Let's review various management types to identify "what we want to be when we grow up." First, let's consider some Bad Boss types.

THE "I WANT EVERYBODY TO LIKE ME" MANAGER

This is typically a person who was promoted into management status too early in his career, beyond his skill set, or simply inappropriately. Therefore, this person already comes armed with somewhat of an inferiority complex, so he wants or needs everyone to like him. Now, there is nothing inherently wrong with wanting to be appreciated and liked in the workplace, but acting in a supervisory capacity *and* wanting to be consistently liked are mutually exclusive. It simply doesn't work effectively, not long term. This manager doesn't want to discipline employees, will avoid employment terminations at any cost, is completely conflict averse, focuses on short-term wins, and, eventually, is easily manipulated by more savvy underlings. It can happen to literally the best of people, who are very likeable and genuine to a fault.

THE "PUFFY-CHESTED IMPOSTER" MANAGER

This is a variation on the theme of those who have been inappropriately thrust into leadership roles, often to the detriment of the general employee population and, on occasion, to the company itself. This manager talks a big game and typically backs it up with an extensive and exhaustive use of charts, graphs, and long-winded epistles about her business accolades, and her eventual rise to success at other places in the professional world. (Please reread that sentence with the sound of wind blowing through your head.) In addition, this manager carefully choreographs any interaction that may be a prelude to a challenge to her expertise and stages that interaction in a public place, with numerous "comrades" present. Disagreement with this manager can be career suicide. Also, if this manager has been brought into the fold from the outside, chances are there are murky areas on her résumé, making fact checking nearly impossible (as all the witnesses to the alleged ascension to greatness are either fabricated or dead).

THE "TYRANT" MANAGER

Most people believe that this form of manager simply doesn't exist in this day and age. How could someone still think it's okay to scream profanities at a subordinate? But we've known of managers who are not afraid of hurling something more substantive, such as a stapler or paperweight or an inbox full of paper at an employee once they've exhausted their string of invectives (it's called "bullying" in today's vernacular). The tyrant has no boundaries, is in complete authority, strikes fear in everyone, and makes no apologies for any action or reaction. This type of manager is an HR nightmare, for obvious reasons. While the other types of managers can be challenges, the tyrant drives and validates bad behavior on a regular basis. Not only is the company prepping for trouble from this activity; others will see and replicate tyranny as their own path to success. HR and upper management must either stop the tyrant cold or they will be left to routinely do damage control and, essentially, clean up the crime scene.

MOJO *from* MASTERS

I (Daren) will never forget the supervisor (we'll call him Steve) who was put in charge of all the newbies in the sales department. Steve was supposed to provide individual performance feedback, to help create individual job goals, and to provide regular one-on-one coaching related to job-specific tasks for each new hire.

What occurred was quite the opposite. Steve never met individually with a new employee—not one. He worked with newbies as a group only. He provided a fill-in-the-blank worksheet for goal setting without direction or individual guidance.

The feedback from new employees in several of the new-hire classes was the same:

- "Steve was nice enough, but he didn't do anything that really helped me."
- "That new-hire program was a joke—and so was Steve. I didn't learn a thing."

(Continued)

- "Our meetings with Steve were a complete waste of time."
- "I learned more about the company from the parking lot attendant than I did from Steve."

A manager like Steve loses all credibility by failing to act on what's expected. Even more disappointing is the fact that Steve had an opportunity to have an extraordinary impact. What a missed opportunity.

Are you as bummed out as we are after reading about those Bad Boss management styles? Enough of that. Let's move on to the Good Boss types.

THE "UNCONDITIONAL LOVE" MANAGER

Ever had a manager who could deliver rotten news (a conversation in which you receive a poor performance review or the management team is told company profits have plummeted) in such a way that you still felt okay afterward? This manager is able to effectively communicate a negative message while keeping the recipient's self-worth intact and, when applicable, is able to propose options for solutions whatever the problem.

We also like to refer to this style as "the sky is the limit" manager because this person is able to do three things effectively:

1. Set high expectations and believe in the employee enough that the employee also begins to believe he can accomplish more.

2. Permit failures along the way, and use those setbacks as learning opportunities for growth. This doesn't mean lowering the standards or accepting the missed mark.

3. Hold employees accountable along the way so that if things aren't going well, the employees see what's coming and aren't surprised by the outcome.

MOJO *from* MASTERS

Straight out of law school, I (Julia) was hired as an associate in a well-respected law firm. The managing partner was the kind of person who was respectful to *everyone* in the firm, used humor in a skillful way at the most appropriate times, and led by example. We all wanted to be at the top of our game because he was. Attorneys and staff alike would laugh and admit that this managing partner could call an employee into his office, fire her, talk her through it, and by the end, she'd walk out thanking *him*.

THE "ADORED" MANAGER

This manager just gets it. And, after working for this manager awhile, you would "follow" her anywhere she leads. She understands that one size does not fit all and crafts every communication, decision, or course of action accordingly—while maintaining a sense of fairness in each decision. Employees know that this manager will *always* do the "right" thing. It may not be a popular decision at the time, but employees have watched this manager and know the decision has been well-reasoned, deliberate, and grounded in consideration of all the information available. Employees would describe this manager as even-handed, fair, and consistent.

THE "GAME OF LIFE" MANAGER

This manager has a more easy-going style. He anticipates that there will be problems and bumps in the road. As a result, he isn't rattled by them. Remember how in the board game *Life* you could land on a square that returned you to start or another that loaded you up with a carful of pink pegs? This manager thrives on such games. He realizes that things are going to happen, works to thwart such dangers, and maintains clarity if the course becomes diverted. He does all this without blaming anyone. He will require employees to glance at the rearview mirror now and again to gain perspective and learn from missed opportunities and/or poor decisions. However, the ultimate focus is always to move forward (even with a carful of pink pegs).

Tips: What else do I need to know?

Clearly, not all managers or all supervisors are created equal, which means they manage differently, work with others differently, and can be managed differently. There are roughly a gazillion books, user's guides, and self-help primers on the market today addressing the topic "how to manage" with little commonality running through them other than the overarching principles of communication skills, leadership skills, and organizational skills. The primary reason is that the job of management requires some customization, since everyone brings unique baggage along for the ride. Our take when it comes to discussing customization is a little different. Although we are advocates for some level of customization to help people reach their individual potential as managers, we'd like to provide you with our own "Top 12 List" of universal truths that apply to everyone who manages people at every level.

Number 12:   Keep your cool.

Number 11:   Listen carefully.

Number 10:   Allow mistakes. Not repeats.

Number 9:   Follow the rules.

Number 8:   Give credit when deserved.

Number 7:   Give direction when needed.

Number 6:   Be truthful. No exceptions.

Number 5:   Get the facts first. React second.

Number 4:   Be respectful—equal doses to everyone.

Number 3:   Require accountability.

Number 2:   Stay above the fray.

Number 1:   Keep your cool (intentionally repeated for effect).

There's one more attribute that we want to pay specific attention to: credibility. We strongly believe that credibility is a key to effectively leading and managing people. Without it, you're sunk. Remember the old adage "Do as I say, not as I do"? Well, forget it. That adage doesn't apply to anyone who manages people. A supervisor's credibility comes not from his title but from the way he acts. There is no quicker way to lose a follower than to say one thing and do the opposite.

Here's one final point about the role of managing people: Managers are dealing with ever-increasing issues of complexity within the workplace, from layers of employment laws and compliance considerations to the unique needs and expectations of a multigenerational workforce. Along with the understanding that we're all required to accomplish more with less. The expectation today for a solid management candidate is that she'll be a tactician, counselor, whip cracker, and number cruncher, along with handling the duties of her day job. If the manager decides to focus on her staff, what does that mean to her own career advancement? How do we, as leaders within our organizations, nurture people to effectively lead others and develop their own successors while growing their own skills? We've got this one. Read on.

Tactics: Where do I go from here?

It's time to take a critical look at our management team (however that is defined within the organization) and ask ourselves some really tough questions. What resources (time, money, and staff) can be allocated for development of our management team? What do we do with managers who are underperforming? How will we pick the next generation of leaders within our organization?

As you wrestle with the answers to those questions, let's

take a look at creating a management training/development program to enhance the management and leadership potential in yourself and the managers in your organization.

CREATION OF A MANAGEMENT DEVELOPMENT PROGRAM

The program can be developed for a specific person or delivered on a larger scale to a group of managers. If developed for a specific manager, the program will entail a customized plan for the individual and may contain many elements similar to those used in an Employee Development Plan (discussed in chapter 5) with the focus obviously on managerial skills. If developed for a group, a training program is typically the chosen methodology.

The goal of a Management Development Program is to provide managers with a clear vision of their role in the organization and to help each manager develop their skills to achieve that vision. Oftentimes, people are promoted to management because they are "good" at what they do. This does not translate automatically to being a "good" manager of people. That is why people benefit significantly from specific direction, a road map if you will, on how to become the next "Manager of the Year."

Several key elements in the development of managers include: (1) teaching managers what works and what doesn't in the development of their own management style; (2) providing tools to foster managers' understanding of working in a collaborative manner and how to get the most from their teams; and (3) helping to develop their leadership attributes so that they earn the respect of team members.

Biz Tip As Gene Mauch puts it, "I'm not the manager because I'm always right, but I'm always right because I'm the manager." NOTE: We included this quote to make you smile. Do not really adopt this quote. Ever.

Let's look closely at these three key elements:

1. **Teaching managers what works and what doesn't.** The goal is to help each manager develop an effective personal management style, which will ultimately be different for each person. Here, we want to help a manager identify personal strengths and weaknesses and build on both. This can be accomplished through a continuous process of review, assessment, and feedback. Often accomplished through 360-degree feedback or similar process, the manager receives feedback on performance from subordinates and peers in the organization, as well as management. In this way, the manager learns how he is perceived by others and learns where he is—or is not—currently working effectively. Action steps are developed to address the areas where weaknesses have been identified.

2. **Providing tools to obtain collaboration.** The objective here is to provide managers with an understanding that they must develop relationships between two ranks within the organization: The first rank is within their own team, and the second rank is networking with other

interrelated groups throughout the company. An effective manager needs to be made aware that an important goal is to bring out the best in the people who report to her. She must be advised that significant effort needs to be made to identify and use the strengths of each individual on the team to allow the entire team to benefit from those strengths. In addition, the manager must work to create relationships with peers throughout the company—a "pay it forward" approach—so that, when the time comes, the manager has built trust with those managers and will be ahead of the curve when asking for their support, involvement, or whatever else is needed.

3. **Developing a manager's leadership attributes.** The target here is to develop the manager's ability to lead and to develop their natural leadership qualities. We can go back to the feedback gathered (in #1) and identify the qualities that come naturally and help the manager understand how to use those skills to lead more effectively. In addition, we can also help the manager by addressing ways to improve qualities that didn't receive high marks. Our hope is that our leaders will gain the ability to lead by example, to lead by positive motivation (not fear), and to lead by "earning" the title. As Mark Twain once said, "Few things are harder to put up with than the annoyance of a good example."

   The methods for developing leadership attributes are limitless. At the top of our list is a mentoring approach. A strong mentor can be an invaluable resource who provides specific, directed guidance to the new or underdeveloped manager. This approach includes the mentor working on specific goals and setting measurable objectives toward achievement of those goals.

Another approach is professional development through training and education specifically focused on leadership and self-awareness. Further training from an expert on leadership can provide concrete action steps for the manager to implement. Yet another approach is to provide managers with a regular forum (internal meeting) in which they discuss the managerial challenges they face and different ways to handle the issues. In this way, they learn from one another. This support-group–like setting serves a distinctive purpose by allowing managers on the same level to vent, discuss, and work together to develop solutions, without the apprehension that might come from engaging in such candor with a group of senior management.

We acknowledge that you are likely reading this and saying to yourself, "That's all well and good, but we've got a job to get done. Who can possibly put these ideas into practice within the confines of an eight-hour workday?" We get it. Our days are the same length as yours. Each of us must prioritize the goals we have for ourselves and our staff, then pick one or two items at a time to work on. Over time, the practices will become part of your culture—second nature, if you will. Then you move on to the next items on your list, and so on, and so on.

BOTTOM LINE

The bottom line is this: Good managers are hard to find and even harder to keep. As we know from experience, people often become managers because they are good at what they do (building widgets, selling cars, fixing furnaces), and they are promoted to management for that reason alone. The only trouble with that methodology is that being good at a job does not automatically equate with being good at managing others in that job. We must provide the tools for success.

By providing tools for success, an organization reflects its belief in the role that managers play in the overall success and continued growth of the business. People who manage people are too important to the future of any business and its ability to attract and retain critical talent. Make sure your managers (or you, as a manager) work on the skills and traits that will develop your inner management style. You'll be so glad you did.

Part IV

EXECUTIONER

Let's close with an in-depth look at one of the toughest managerial tasks—the "execution" of the employment termination process (a.k.a. the employment "death sentence").

CHAPTER 10

Dismissed, Displaced & Whacked—Oh My!

TERMINATION AS A SECOND LANGUAGE

By failing to prepare, you are preparing to fail.
—Benjamin Franklin

Eventually termination of employment affects *everybody*. Odds are that you will be the one either delivering the message or receiving the message at some point in your professional career.

Obviously, neither role is fun to play, but for the sake of argument, let's focus on your role as the one conducting the employment termination. Bear in mind that we are not talking about employee-initiated terminations here. You know, the straightforward kind in which you accept the departing employee's letter of resignation or retirement, throw a send-off celebration, and prepare a job advertisement for their replacement. We are talking about good old-fashioned, involuntary terminations along the lines of "You're not doing your job" or "You're not coming to work on time," or "You're simply not cutting it." Or even worse, the underlying reason is that "The boss hates you, and I am left to dream up a reason to fire you."

MOJO *from* MASTERS

To the above point, *never ever* make up a "reason" to fire someone. Even if the truth hurts, it needs to be said. It is much better to be honest about the basis for a termination than to try and prevent hurt feelings by sugarcoating or fabricating a reason. Give the employee the benefit of knowing the real reason: "The boss doesn't like you because you slap him on the back and call him 'buddy' every time you see him." In this way, you may help the employee avoid making the same mistake in future employment. Please keep in mind this is also important because a made-up reason could look like a pretext or a cover-up for an underlying impermissible motive (that is, a discriminatory reason) for the termination. Don't inadvertently create such an impression because you are otherwise trying to protect the employee from having their feelings hurt.

As with nearly everything in the workplace today, the way we handle terminating employees has changed for the better in most businesses. Guidelines for how to appropriately handle termination situations are plentiful. However, for managers to actually take the time to find and use those guidelines seems to be an insurmountable task. Add to the equation an unskilled or apathetic manager who is part of the termination process, and the organization may have potentially derailed the desired outcome.

That desired outcome, in case you are wondering, is a peaceful and brief dialogue between the company representative and the soon-to-be terminated employee, detailing the elements of the separation and expediting their vacating the premises, all in a legally supported and professional manner.

Why should it matter how the termination is processed and how the conversation is handled? Let's just say that it matters—a lot. As with every task we undertake in the workplace, we must work at it. Our goal for you is to have a better understanding of the pitfalls present in an employment-termination situation and how to avoid those pitfalls. We truly want to make termination conversations a "second language" for you, meaning that your fluency in the communication itself and your understanding of the factors involved will become sharpened.

> *Biz Tip*   Given the multiple layers of legal protection for employees today, it is imperative that anyone faced with the task of terminating an employee be well prepared.

Tales: Am I the only sane person in the room?

Across the board, it is safe to say that no one *enjoys* ending the employment of another person. Contrary to popular opinion,

HR professionals (the ones usually burdened with the task of doing the firing or at least designated to be in the room while the supervisor does) do care about people—tremendously. It's why the person went into the HR profession to begin with. "Why did I choose HR? Because I am a 'people person' and I love working with people."

Before we address the right way to do things (and help you become fluent in this new second language), let's check in one last time with Bad Boss, from whom we can learn so much.

THE BOSS WHO IS ALL TALK, NO ACTION

Bad Boss opens the meeting with a lengthy and protracted introduction, starting with, "Thanks for coming here today. We haven't talked in a while. How are Carole and the kids? How is that soccer team you're coaching?" Yes, I (Daren) actually heard Bad Boss put a pink-slip-recipient-in-waiting through such blather. The employee was remarkably gracious, answered the cocktail party questions, and then waited for the other shoe to drop. More inane pleasantries were exchanged between the two about the company, their history together, the community, their family activities, and so on for *thirty minutes!* For those of you who have conducted employee termination meetings, you know this is defined as an eternity. (Once again, I was besieged by a floating-over-the-room, complete out-of-body experience.) When the conversation was over, Bad Boss thanked the employee again for coming to the meeting, and the employee and I walked out of the conference room together. The employee was not fired by Bad Boss in the meeting. Only when we arrived back at the employee's office did I find out via text that I was to fire him. Well played, Bad Boss!

THE BOSS WITH A BIG HEART

Surely there are worse things than a boss with a big heart. Agreed. But "boss with a big heart" is not so helpful when it comes to unsavory tasks like firing someone. In this situation, Bad Boss is a nice (a.k.a. milquetoast) manager who has been told he must fire his assistant—for theft. This is a for-cause termination because the discharge is based on the employee's own bad conduct. Others in the company have conducted an investigation and determined that theft occurred at the hands of this employee. Bad Boss is reluctant to move forward with the termination. Despite the evidence, he simply doesn't believe that the employee would act that way and thinks a second chance should be given. However, under company policy, this is about as straightforward as it gets: The employee violated company policy and the policy states that an employee will be subject to immediate termination for this particular offense.

As you may have anticipated, the meeting begins badly because the employee enters the room visibly upset, intuitive enough to know something is coming. (Really, truly. You enter a room with your boss and someone from HR with a file folder. It's pretty easy to see something's coming, right?) Bad Boss tells employee of the termination of employment based on the company's determination that the employee stole from the company. Keep in mind that the employee also could see this coming since he was involved in the underlying investigation and has been on paid leave pending the outcome of the investigation.

No sooner is that over than Boss apologizes to the employee for the company's insensitive decision, and even offers to provide the employee with a reference letter. Boss continues to placate the employee by adding, "This was not my decision; if it were I would keep you, and give you a second chance." Boss closes with negative dialogue about the company. In the span of a few moments, the employee has shifted from being fearful and contrite over the matter to being angry and aggressive. Bad Boss has undermined the company's decision by characterizing the termination as harsh and unforgiving. This impression is solely due to the picture painted by the overly apologetic boss. The company did not "owe" the employee a second chance. The credibility of the company and the HR process was compromised at the hands of Bad Boss, who failed to execute the task with appropriate discretion.

Biz Tip If Bad Boss truly had reservations about the validity of the investigation or its result, Bad Boss should have taken that up with management when he was told to fire the employee. It would have been prudent for Bad Boss to look further if he had a legitimate reason to question the basis of the termination. However, all of that inquiry needs to be carried out prior to the actual firing. In this way, if the firing is ultimately deemed unwarranted, a more suitable resolution can be reached and communicated to the employee. The termination meeting itself is neither the time nor the place to dispute the firing decision.

THE BOSS WITH SWAGGER

Finally there is the boss who has swagger—but only in a crowd. In our final setting, Bad Boss has decided he doesn't like the employee, thinks he is a mediocre performer at best, and wants him gone. The routine process of setting goals and expectations, followed by tracking performance and coaching for improvement when needed, has been completely cast aside. Bad Boss has some swagger to display, and no blankety-blank process is getting in the way.

A meeting is set, and the employee and others are slightly circumspect about it (since the boss is attending), but no one could guess what is about to unfold. The group meets. Bad Boss decides to advise employee of her discharge during the meeting, truly enhancing how special the moment is and setting a wonderful, morale-boosting workplace environment going forward. Not.

During the course of the discussion, the boss makes it clear that the employee has to go effective immediately, yet mercilessly he doesn't end the meeting. The employee stays in the meeting, awkwardly waiting for who knows what. At the close of the meeting, the employee follows the HR representative to his office to ask the embarrassing and not-so-obvious question: "Did I really just get fired? In front of everyone?" The act of terminating an employee is difficult enough, but with an audience? We can do better.

Also keep in mind that the termination process has a certain degree of the unknown to it. As we've stated and underscored throughout this book, that unknown element, in this termination process and many other HR functions, is the human element. In an employment termination, the human element involves the unpredictable reaction of the soon-to-be-terminated employee.

Let's discuss pregame strategies that may assist in diffusing the hard-to-predict human element in the equation.

Tips: What else do I need to know?

Let's start with the premise that there are numerous ways to handle the communication of a discharge to an employee, with varying levels of success. What is critical for those handling the termination is to be thorough in evaluating the discharge decision, then to be well prepared for the discussion itself. We can share with you the following pointers based on years of collective experience—both in the trenches (being the communicators of the termination message) and in defense of companies whose communications are later being scrutinized with overwhelming intensity (either as retold in a deposition or at trial).

ANALYZE THE RISK ASSOCIATED WITH THE DISCHARGE BEFORE LOWERING THE HAMMER

We must start with analyzing the basis for the employment discharge. Begin by reviewing all applicable company policies, procedures, and relevant precedent-setting events. Don't forget to determine whether the employee is an employee-at-will or has an employment contract. All actions must be consistent with the requirements in the contract, if one is in place, as well as consistent with the policies and procedures of the company. Similar underlying facts and circumstances in relation to the current discharge should also be considered since they may serve to establish a precedent for handling those matters.

The discharge must also be in compliance with applicable federal, state, and local employment laws. There is a legal minefield to be skillfully managed. Keep in mind the alphabet soup of employment laws: FLSA, FMLA, ADAAA, ADEA, EEO (Title VII), IRCA, GINA, OSHA. There are many legal considerations. Be careful! To analyze whether there is risk inherent in the termination decision or whether there are other risks present, one should ask a number of questions, including those in the box that follows.

BE WELL INFORMED BEFORE DECIDING WHETHER TO FIRE AN EMPLOYEE

1. **Is the employee a member of a protected category?**

   If the employee is in a protected category, you don't need to alter your decision. There is, however, inherent risk under such circumstances. Evaluate whether any additional steps are required. For example, if the employee has a disability, there may be a need to go through an accommodation analysis before moving forward.

2. **Is the timing of the discharge inherently suspect?**

   If the decision to discharge falls immediately after the employee has raised an internal complaint, or perhaps participated in an investigation, or exercised some other protected right, the intervening basis for the termination decision must be closely evaluated.

3. **Is the termination decision based on a good reason?**

   It doesn't really have to be. Employment-at-will says a person can be fired for any reason or no reason at all, so long as it is not an *unlawful* reason. This means that *dumb* or *silly* reasons for firing an employee are not necessarily prohibited. The *sillier* the reason for termination, however, the more suspect the basis for the termination. "I was fired for wearing yellow tennis shoes"—really? Yellow tennis shoes are not protected by law, but this opens the door for greater scrutiny.

   (Continued)

4. Has the employee recently pursued or filed for workers' compensation benefits, blown the whistle on inappropriate or unlawful activity by the company, raised an internal complaint of allegedly unlawful activity, or otherwise engaged in protected activity?

   Retaliation claims are on the rise. Employers need to evaluate adverse actions against employees in light of all the circumstances present.

5. Has the employee recently exercised any rights under any of the employment laws listed in the alphabet soup (for example, FLSA, FMLA, ADA, etc.)? Filed for bankruptcy? Requested an accommodation for a disability? Had their wages recently garnished?

   Prior to a termination we must look at all the circumstances that surround the particular employee. A discharge decision can't be made in a vacuum. You may ultimately decide the termination is warranted and sound, despite some inherent risk. It becomes a question of risk management at that point.

When in doubt, seek outside legal counsel to discuss all the circumstances surrounding the proposed employment termination to determine whether the company is on solid ground. You cannot be too careful in this area. It will be the best money ever spent. Promise.

MAINTAIN THE FIRED EMPLOYEE'S DIGNITY THROUGHOUT THE PROCESS

Do not underestimate the importance of this point. More often than not, if an employee feels slighted, affronted, or disrespected during the process, the matter often escalates into a demand letter, administrative claim, or worse. This result occurs because the employee now has an emotional ax to grind, which can cloud rational thinking.

It can be difficult, but work mightily to help the employee maintain dignity during the departure. This means giving serious consideration to things like the timing of the discussion (for instance, prior to the start of the workday or after hours), whether to allow the employee to gather personal items immediately or return during nonwork hours, and by whom the message should be delivered (an archenemy is not the best choice).

CLEARLY COMMUNICATE THE REASON FOR THE TERMINATION OF EMPLOYMENT

Make it clear to the employee that the company has reached a decision that the employee's employment is ending. State the basis for the discharge decision—succinctly and only once. We need to be clear, but the point doesn't need repeating. Write it out. Practice. Really.

If the bearer of the termination news gets even a little nervous, or if the pink-slip recipient becomes emotional, there is a natural tendency to repeat one's message or fill the anxiety-ridden room with blather. Avoid that tendency. Once you've communicated the discharge message, the employee isn't really listening anymore. He's moved to thoughts of, "Where will I find another job?" or "What will I tell my wife and kids?" or "What about the mortgage?" This isn't easy.

Move on to the administrative matters to be handled such as return of keys and security badges, retrieval of company-provided equipment, COBRA and benefits communications, and payment of the final paycheck.

Remember to hold firm. This is not a "discussion" about the discharge decision itself. The employee may take issue with the discharge and immediately start ranting in defense of his behavior, or making comparisons to employees he believes were treated less harshly, or offering justifications and excuses for his job performance. Listen to the employee, but don't get drawn into a battle over who's right or wrong. You will need to be considerate but firm. Explain that all the circumstances have been assessed and the decision stands.

AVOID SURPRISES

In a perfect world, a termination conversation is not a surprise. The point here is that when we must fire an employee—say, for poor performance—we should have had prior conversations with the individual in which she has been informed of her performance deficiencies and given specific tasks/goals to accomplish in order to improve. Follow-up and feedback should have been given as to whether sufficient improvement was made. Along that continuum, the employee should have been warned about the consequences (including potential termination of employment) if her job performance didn't improve. In this way, the employee is not surprised when handed a pink slip because the lack of satisfactory performance or improvement of the same has been made clear to her along the way.

BE COMPASSIONATE WITHOUT BEING APOLOGETIC OR EMOTIONAL

Right from the start of the conversation, it is best to minimize the chitchat and move quickly to the decision. Start by letting the employee know that the decision was difficult (or whatever other adjective may be appropriate) but that the company has decided to end the employment relationship. It can be tough to anticipate what the employee's reaction may be. Therefore, you need to be prepared for anything (tears, silence, anger, disbelief, indignation, grief, shock, stoicism, indifference, or perhaps several emotions in combination).

An employee who senses there is some level of compassion from the company will "feel" better than the employee who senses only that the company has turned its back on him. This message is best delivered by using a calm and professional tone and communicating a sense that the company cares about the employee as a person, but is no longer able to continue the employment relationship.

The table is now set. It's time to engage in the final prep work for the discharge conversation. By developing a well-defined process for handling employment terminations and communicating the same, you will eliminate guesswork and possibly minimize the impact of the unpredictable factors.

Tactics: Where do I go from here?

As we create the actual process, let's start by beginning with the end in mind. We intend to have a solid termination process in which we follow our own policies, procedures, and precedents; establish a legally sound review of pending employee terminations; and promote a stable workplace environment for the remaining staff.

To achieve this, the most effective employment termination process includes the four elements described below.

1. **Pre-termination preparation.** We have addressed the importance of preparation throughout this chapter. We are talking about doing one's homework prior to every employment termination. You may use the Employment Discharge Checklist, set forth on page 179, as a road map to review and analyze a termination decision prior to "executing" on it.

2. **Determine suitable logistics.** Select a location, preferably not in a high-traffic area of the office, in which the confidentiality of the conversation is ensured. As for a suggested time of day or day of the week that is best for such conversations, our preference is to make that determination on a case-by-case and not make it predictable (don't create a stigma such as "black Fridays"). Keep in mind, you may have unique circumstances that necessitate the termination meeting to be held off-site. Don't pick a public venue such as restaurant or coffee shop for the off-site conversation. Under very rare circumstances, a termination conversation may be held by phone.

3. **Conduct the "term" meeting.** We are providing you with a few examples of discharge conversations, but obviously it must be customized for each situation. We hope it provides you with some vocabulary to use to improve your fluency in termination as a second language.

COMMUNICATING THE EMPLOYMENT DISCHARGE

To communicate the discharge decision:

- ☑ Offer brief welcome.

- ☑ Let the employee know the company has carefully reviewed the situation and has had to make a difficult decision.

- ☑ Inform the employee of the termination.

- ☑ State the basis/reason for the termination.

- ☑ Acknowledge the challenging, difficult nature of the situation.

- ☑ Move to business items (COBRA/insurance matters, employment verification and/or references, discussion of any "open" business and its handling, etc.).

- ☑ Make arrangements for return of company items (keys, computers, cell phone, company car, etc.).

- ☑ Determine best way to remove personal items from the employee's workspace/office.

- ☑ Explain the follow-up communication that will be coming (final paycheck, employee benefits, etc.).

- ☑ Close the meeting; allow for as graceful an exit as possible.

Scenario I: Employee fired for poor performance

Executioner (HR): Hi, Sammy. I appreciate you meeting with me this afternoon.

Sammy: Sure. What's up?

Executioner (HR): As you are aware, we've been discussing your job performance for several months now.

Sammy: Yeah. I think things are definitely looking better.

Executioner (HR): Well, the performance deficiencies that we've discussed have actually not gotten any better. We've given you several months to improve, but that hasn't happened to our satisfaction. We have decided to end your employment with the company, effective today.

Sammy: Come on! I've been trying really hard, and my skills are improving daily. Haven't you been looking at my numbers?

Executioner (HR): Actually, we have been watching your numbers closely, and there has been no real improvement. I have reports from the last three months since we put you on warning. You have not achieved the goal in any of the three months, nor have you engaged in any of the other activities we requested such as job training at two different machines, becoming certified at the lead bench, or doing any of the online training courses recommended by your department lead.

Sammy: This is B.S.! You guys aren't paying attention! Numbers, schmumbers! (*Sammy is getting visibly agitated and angry.*)

Executioner (HR): We have given this very serious consideration. We believe we provided a meaningful opportunity for you to improve over the past three months. Your department lead and the training manager both spent extra time working with you. This shouldn't really come as a surprise since we discussed in your last performance meeting that all of the items still needed significant work.

This decision is final. I have your final paycheck, as well as an exit package that discusses benefit continuation. You will also receive benefit information in the mail. You can leave your security card with me. I don't think you have any tools here, is that right?

Sammy: Yup. This whole thing stinks!

Executioner (HR): I understand. A situation like this is difficult. (*Slight pause*) If you have any questions later, you may contact me by phone. (*Another pause*) Why don't I walk out with you?

Sammy: Oh, sure, now you think I'm gonna do something bad.

Executioner (HR): No, I actually just think it's the right thing to do.

EMPLOYMENT DISCHARGE CHECKLIST

To evaluate the discharge decision:

- ☑ Review the personnel file and all documentation related to the termination.

- ☑ Evaluate the relevant company policies and procedures (progressive discipline, performance management).

- ☑ Determine whether the information provided as the basis/reason for the termination is valid.

- ☑ Verify employment-at-will status; look for any employment contract, offer letter, or other written communication stating length of employment or related terms.

(Continued)

☑ Check (and double-check) the legal/compliance requirements. Have the decision reviewed by legal counsel.

☑ Create your agenda for the discharge meeting.

☑ Reserve a place to meet with the employee; select the most appropriate time and day.

☑ Book the meeting with any additional required attendees.

☑ Determine the security issues (employee access to building, computers, etc.) prior to meeting with the employee.

☑ Calculate and prepare the final paycheck (check applicable state laws).

☑ Determine whether a severance payment and/or a release will be provided.

☑ Determine several options for the employee to retrieve personal items.

☑ Determine how the open job will be staffed in the short and long term.

☑ Arrange for IT to disable the employee's access to company systems.

☑ Prepare the communication to be given to the relevant staff post-separation, as well as a plan for delivering the message.

Scenario II: Employee fired for unacceptable performance and a bad attitude

Executioner (HR): Good afternoon, Clara. Thank you for meeting with me this afternoon.

Clara: Sure. Like I really had a choice.

Executioner (HR): Clara, the reason I asked to meet with you is to discuss your employment. We have decided, after significant consideration, that we must end your employment with the company.

Clara: Holy s*#@! This place is a joke. You've got to be kidding me, right?

Executioner (HR): This is no joke, and no one has taken this decision lightly.

Clara: Let's get to brass tacks: I get my job done and come to work every day. You can't fire me.

Executioner (HR): We are ending your employment on the basis of your refusal to perform required job duties and your unacceptable attitude toward the company, your job, your supervisor, and your coworkers. You refuse to perform job assignments that you don't like, such as sweeping and cleaning the machines in your area, which is required of everyone in the department. You regularly state that you hate this company and your job. And you consistently yell and raise your voice with your supervisor and your coworkers.

Clara: That's no reason to fire me. Other people are worse than me. What about Tim and Stephanie? Their attitudes really stink.

Executioner (HR): We are here to talk about you, not Tim and Stephanie. We have spoken with you about this at each performance review, and you've been written up on seven different occasions over the last two years for these issues.

Clara: So why now? It's probably because I just came back from workers' compensation leave. You guys hate that.

Executioner (HR): This decision is based solely on your refusal to perform your required job duties, your harsh attitude with coworkers, and your insubordination with supervisors. As you know, on Tuesday of this week, you had another run-in with your supervisor in which you refused to clean the lathe machine and threw the cleaning supplies on the ground. That incident was the final straw.

Clara: I'm not buyin' it.

Executioner (HR): Also, since you raised the issue of workers' compensation, I want to address it. It is important to clarify that your workers' compensation claim had no bearing on this decision. That matter was resolved over two years ago. In fact, your current supervisor who recommended your termination was not here at that time and wouldn't have any knowledge of that.

Clara: It's still bogus.

Executioner (HR): Let's talk for just another minute. I have your final paycheck for you. I also have some benefits information in this envelope. You'll receive another mailing about benefits within the next week. I need for you to return your backdoor key.

Clara: Here's your stupid key. Look here, I know a lawyer, and this isn't the last word from me.

Executioner (HR): At this time it's probably best for me to walk back with you to the work area so you can grab your belongings and then leave.

Clara: I don't have anything back there. I just want to say a few good-byes.

Executioner (HR): Sorry, it will be extremely disruptive while everyone is working. I'll just walk you to the front door, then, and you can hold those good-byes until later.

Clara: More of the same. This place is nuts! I can see myself to the door!

HR still escorts Clara out the front door. A few people from HR later walk through the parking lot to ensure that Clara has departed the premises.

4. **Post-meeting activity.** After the meeting is over, have someone walk the employee to his desk to grab necessary items and depart or to pack up his personal items and then depart the building. To "escort" an employee through this part of the process (particularly a long-time employee) can be demoralizing to the employee, so be careful in the execution of this process. This is where we need to customize the process to make it the most palatable approach for the employee while protecting the company's interests. It is not easy, but work hard to avoid an embarrassing or patronizing situation for the terminated employee.

It can be a delicate balance, but too many times an

employee has taken something that doesn't belong to them (corporate documents, books, records, files), or sent a terse email to the masses (on the way out the door), or even destroyed company property in anger. Don't let it happen. Make sure the company's assets are protected and the terminated employee is tactfully walked to the door. Keep in mind that the retrieval of items and packing a box may be remarkably painful or humiliating. Consequently, it may be a task better left for another day (the following weekend or an evening after work hours).

We have never been big fans of terminated employees going on a building-wide "good-bye tour" to talk with their colleagues. If they want to meet after hours, fine, but the termination is already disrupting the business, and the tour only makes that situation worse.

Later, someone will need to communicate with the employees who are impacted by the departure (same department, work group, etc.) that the employee is no longer working at the company. There is *no* need to detail the reason(s) for the employment separation; simply focus on the business impact in terms of who will be picking up certain responsibilities, new reporting structure, or any other work-related matter. You want to focus the employees on moving forward in a positive manner, not on the circumstances related to their newly terminated colleague.

Biz Tip We tend to worry about the negative effect that an employment termination may have on the remaining staff. It is a reasonable concern, naturally, and we do want to alleviate any unnecessary uncertainty ("Am I next?"). However, we also need to give the remaining employees credit. They may actually agree with the termination decision ("It's about time the company fired her . . . she never came to work on time!").

BOTTOM LINE

Implementing an effective termination process is a *key* to defensible risk management for the business. The failure to do so can damage the credibility and sustainability of the business internally as well as with customers, vendors, and the marketplace. By taking the time to be prepared and to fully understand how to conduct a legally compliant termination, you can provide an ongoing valuable service to the organization. You will want to follow the pointers we've provided. First, ask the tough questions about the underlying basis for the termination and be sure you are satisfied with the answers. Second, plan mightily for the termination conversation and meeting. Be sure to practice the termination conversation by yourself at least once. Take the time to plan carefully and then prepare yourself for the unexpected. You'll be so glad you did.

Conclusion

So, there you have it. Our goal in writing this book was to enlighten, to educate, and—we hope—to entertain you, for the world of human-capital management is a deep and wide expanse from which to draw. By blending humor with practical tools for application, we were focusing on bringing you closer to situations from your own workplace while giving you ideas and processes to put into practice. At its fundamental core, *Lifeguard, Babysitter, Executioner* is really just a book about *people*. That's what makes this topic so fascinating.

People are the greatest variable (and most valuable asset) in the workplace—period. You can argue market conditions, product placement, and operational best practices ad nauseam, but your reliance on people in the workplace (colleagues, subordinates, superiors) will *never* be a constant. Why? The answer is the existence of any combination of factors, including employee attitudes, experience, expectations, generational issues, workplace environment, peers, customers, job location, compensation, professional growth, industry type, boredom, anger, jealousy—pretty much any variable you can come up with. Given these varying factors, it is understandable why those who manage, or those who simply work with other people, often feel that they are required to wear multiple hats and perform multiple duties at any given moment. The multiple hats (and related duties) of Lifeguard, Babysitter, and Executioner are yours for the making. Take comfort. You will wear them well.

Index

About the Authors

Daren Fristoe

As president of The Fristoe Group, a provider of human resource solutions for small to midsized businesses, Daren Fristoe has been a corporate downsizer, a bailout adviser, and an executive enrichment coach.

During his professional career, he has been "in the rooms" where we wish the walls could talk, and he brings the insights gathered from those experiences to the printed page. Daren has had responsibilities for the overall management of varied disciplines, including human resources, corporate operations, training and education, benefits and salary administration, general office management, franchise services, communication, corporate marketing and event management, and community service outreach programs.

Prior to forming TFG, Daren worked in the industries of collision-repair franchising, e-commerce procurement, telecommunications, staffing, international manufacturing, and property and casualty insurance. In addition to those industries, the TFG client roster includes organizations from the worlds of architecture, engineering, banking, health care, commercial development, customer service centers, and local governmental departments.

Daren enjoys spending time with his wife, Jody, their son, Adam, and their daughter, Emma. He also has a passion for community service and fills multiple leadership roles in his hometown of Lee's Summit, Missouri.

After receiving his bachelor of arts in political science from the University of Missouri at Columbia, he earned his juris doctor from the University of Tulsa College of Law.

Julia Riggle McKee

Julia "Julie" McKee serves as general counsel with an international medical device company headquartered in Kansas City where she oversees legal, compliance, and human resources matters. Previously, as an owner and the president of FBD Consulting, LLC, a human resources consulting firm, Julia specialized in HR policy and procedure development, corporate training, HR audits, compliance on employment-related matters, and conducting internal investigations. She worked with a number of private and public companies, such as Dine Equity (IHOP & Applebee's), Garmin, Layne Christensen, and National

Financial Partners. Earlier in her career, Julia was a partner with the national law firm, Stinson Morrison Hecker (now Stinson Leonard Street), where she handled employment law defense work, including litigation, along with compliance advice and counsel. She worked on a number of employment law cases and was involved in the defense of one of the first same-sex sexual harassment lawsuits in the country. While at the law firm, she also served as associate general counsel for employment matters and was the chairperson of the Human Resource Consulting Practice Group. Julia is an entertaining and well-respected speaker on human resources, employment law, and corporate compliance topics.

Julia enjoys spending time with her husband, Mark, and their three daughters, Mallory, Chandler, and Brooke. Julia prefers the outdoors: boating, waterskiing, snow skiing, biking, and cheering from the sidelines of her daughters' activities. She is also an avid University of Kansas basketball fan—Rock Chalk Jayhawk! She has a passion for worthwhile causes and has served on the board of several charities and cofounded an annual celebrity fund-raiser for a local children's hospital. She volunteers in the community with her daughters through the National Charity League.

Julia graduated with Distinction from the University of Kansas with a bachelor of arts degree. She earned a double major in Personnel Administration and Communications. Julia was awarded her juris doctor degree with Dean's honors from Washburn University School of Law.